The Real St. Nicholas

Very best wishes
from Louise Carus
2002

The Real St. Nicholas

Tales of Generosity and Hope from around the World

Louise Carus
Editor and Translator

Wheaton, Illinois ♦ Chennai (Madras), India

The Theosophical Society acknowledges with gratitude the generous support of the Kern Foundation in the publication of this book.

First Quest Edition 2002

The Theosophical Publishing House
P. O. Box 270
Wheaton, IL 60189-0270

A publication of the Theosophical Publishing House,
a department of the Theosophical Society in America

Cover and text design and typesetting by Beth Hansen-Winter

Library of Congress Cataloging-in-Publication Data

The real St. Nicholas: tales of generosity and hope from around the world / Louise Carus, translator and editor.
p. cm.
Includes bibliographical references.
ISBN 0-8356-0813-1
1. Santa Claus. 2. Nicholas, Saint, Bp. of Myra—Legends. 3. Tales. I. Carus, Louise.
GT4992 .R43 2002
394.2663—dc21

2002066752

5 4 3 2 1 * 02 03 04 05 06

Printed in Hong Kong through Global Interprint, Santa Rosa, California

Dedicated to a renewed love of the real St. Nicholas of Myra
and to a rebuilding of his church in Manhattan
as a shrine of reflection and remembrance for all peoples

Groeten van St. Nicolaas

Contents

Acknowledgments

First, I want to thank my uncle Alwin Carus, who fondly remembers St. Nicholas coming to his home on December 5 and 6 before World War I. More recently, he and I have celebrated St. Nicholas's Feast Day with Jessica, Lindsey, and Chelsea Reidies for several years. They were the first, with their parents and grandparents, to hear some of our St. Nicholas stories in English. They were so responsive that I was inspired to translate a few new stories each year.

In preparing for and writing this book, Susan Rublaitus has pressed me on and helped me beyond words. I am very grateful for her friendship and enthusiastic support. Giesela von der Goltz provided hospitality in Munich and introduced me to our Czech friend, Vladimira Plecakova, who took me to Prague and was invaluable there. Dr. Edward Tick led an inspiring journey to the St. Nicholas Monastery in the mountains of Crete. Ed's deep understanding of Greek history and culture opened many doors for me. In Switzerland, the Zürich St. Nicholas Society was helpful in sharing their experience in serving in the spirit of St. Nicholas in the community prisons and hospitals and to others in need. The Swiss Küssnacht am Rigi St. Nicholas Society gave us support and encouragement as well. Very special thanks to Marydale Stewart

---

The Circle of Love *by* Eliza *Manning*, *from* Coming of Father Christmas

and her staff at the public library in Peru, Illinois, for assistance far beyond the call of duty. Several friends at St. Bede Abbey and Academy in Peru have also been most cooperative: Father Gabriel Bullock has helped throughout this project with wise suggestions and generous support. He traveled to Myra in Turkey and to St. Nicholas's church there and followed the development of this book over the years. Father Dominic also assisted in lending a valuable resource book, and Father Claude Peifer shared his knowledge of Greek. Father Ronald Margherio offered insider details about Bari, Italy, and its famous Basilica dedicated to St. Nicholas. Father Gregory Buss of St. George Orthodox Church in Spring Valley, Illinois, and Rev. Stephen Martz of St. Nicholas Church in Elk Grove Village, Illinois, assisted in compiling lists of St. Nicholas churches throughout the United States. Father Aloys von Euw, in the Swiss Alps, is a living, practicing follower of St. Nicholas who allowed me to study in his extensive library of St. Nicholas literature in Morschach near Lucerne. What fun it was! Thanks also to Mara-Lee Rosenbarger for library help.

Sharron Dorr at Quest Books has been invaluable as friend, professional storyteller, editor, and publisher. Together, we have polished the stories from my translations and have tried to be faithful to the originals as we found them in the German language. I am very grateful as well to Brenda Rosen, also with Quest, who helped conceptualize the book's structure. Betty Lou Willand tested the stories with me in local schools. She has continued to help with countless other details, including giving our three recipes a final test, with most tasty results! Elisabeth Cominos in Athens helped us with final Greek permissions, not to mention the hospitality shown by her and her husband, Achilles, while I was in Greece.

Many thanks to Sherwood Sugden of the *Monist Journal* and to Margaret Madelung, who found the painting of St. Nicholas as the Healer in Budapest. Ed Krolak of our Illinois Valley Community College told me about the church of St. Nicholas in Yarmouth, England, founded in 1119—almost nine hundred years ago! Countless acquaintances from all over the map have had their own stories to tell about St. Nicholas. I'm thinking in particular of Pat Trompeter,

who gave me a good source. In Crete, Father Chariton, Fragradakis Mixales, and Panagrotis Milonakis all kindly shared their true stories of how, even today, St. Nicholas heals and rescues. I also want to acknowledge Ethel Vogelsang and Ruth Ammann, my great friends in Zürich, who were willing and able to jump in and help out whenever needed. Finally, special thanks go to Blouke Carus, Marianne Carus, Cele Carus, and Paul Carus for their warm support, and to Win Carus as well, who graciously helped with the translation of some of the foreign words in "The Russian Icon."

Thank you, everyone, for assisting us to get this book published in 2002. Believe it or not, today as I write, it is the twentieth of the second month in the year 2002!

SWEDEN
Holy Night
A Small Fish Story
IRELAND
St. Nicholas
Retrieves
the Ball
NETHERLANDS
The Pfeffernüsse
GERMANY
St. Nicholas Buys a Young
Man His Freedom
FRANCE
Anticipation
The Nine Questions
SPAIN
St. Nicholas
and the Ant
ITALY
BARI
The site of
St. Nicholas's
grave since
1087 AD.
The
Miller's Tail
The Sick King
and the Simpleto

The St. Nicholas Map
FINLAND
St. Nicholas and the Monster
ESTONIA
The Beautiful Crop of Rye
RUSSIA
Marko, the Rich Man
UKRAINE
The Devil's Wager
ROMANIA
St. Nicholas Finds the Path
The Money Bag of Molsch Talpasch
The Icon's Warm Bread
The Healing Oil
TURKEY
The Hermit and the Mouse Maiden
Demre (Myra)
The home of St. Nicholas
N
Daniel T. Doolin

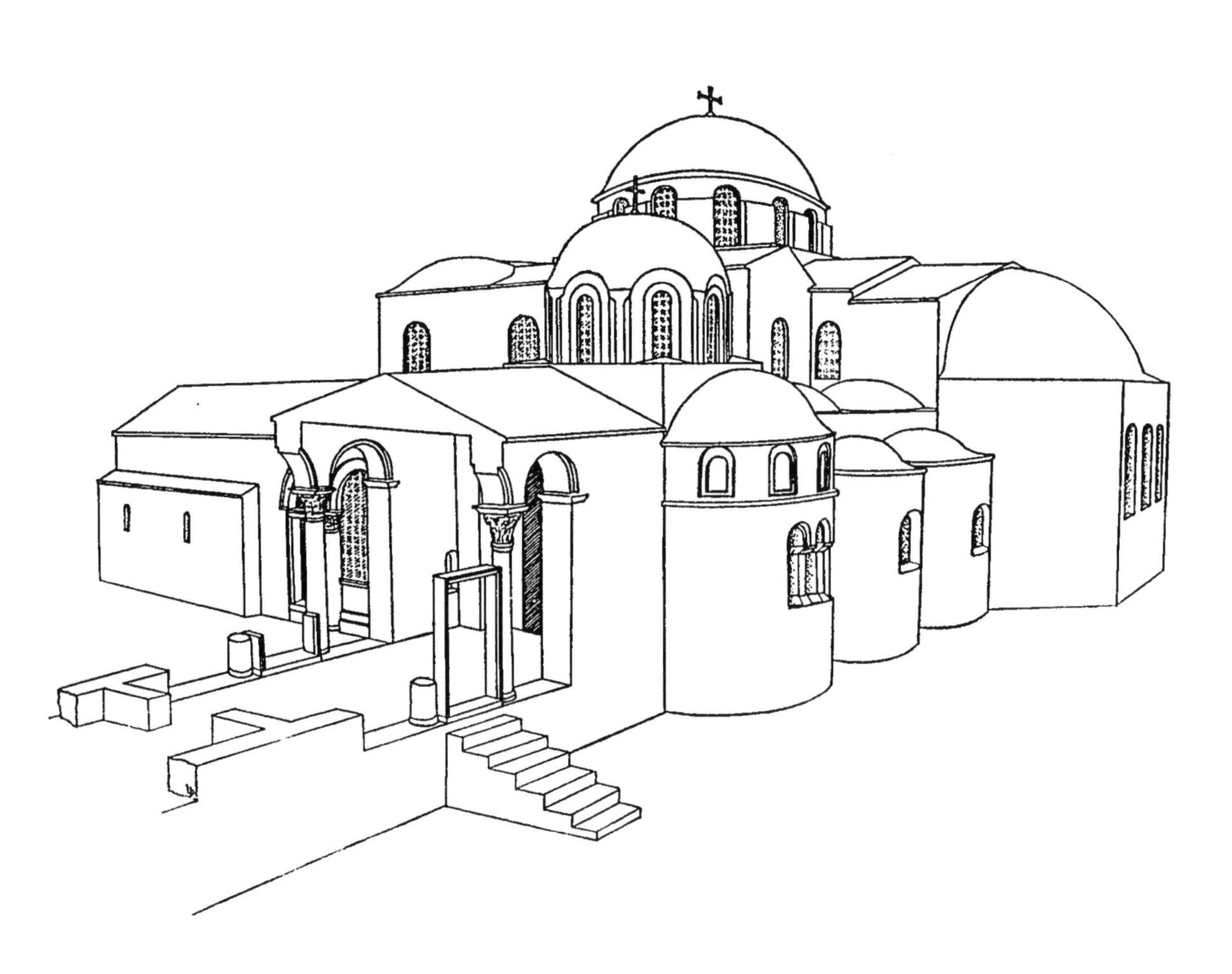

Introduction

Once there was a child who had many questions about Santa Claus. We also have had many questions, and so we have read books and traveled to different countries and talked with many people to find the answers. Now we would like to share with you what we have learned. The first thing is that the name "Santa Claus," which comes from the Dutch *Sinterklaas*, is really a nickname. The real man has long been thought of as an early Christian saint named Nicholas. Over the centuries, he has become known as the patron saint of sailors, travelers, bakers, bankers and businessmen, lawyers and jurists, prisoners and prison guards, pawn brokers, millers and grain traders, pharmacists, maidens, brides, couples, and—most especially—of children. Let us start at the beginning, then, with something about the life of the real Saint Nicholas.

Long ago, in the fourth century A.D., Nicholas was a bishop in Myra, a city in the province of Lycia on the northeastern shores of the Mediterranean Sea, in what was then called Asia Minor. Today, Myra has been renamed Demre, in modern Turkey. You can still visit St. Nicholas's church there, which has been restored many times in the last sixteen hundred years. It is one of the oldest churches in the world, and if you visit its garden, you will find a large statue of St. Nicholas with statues of children from different countries around the world encircling him.

Line drawing of Saint Nicholas Church, Myra, Turkey, as it appeared during the Byzantine era

St. Nicholas Church as it looks today in Demre (formerly Myra), Turkey

Although St. Nicholas lived and was buried in Myra, his grave was later moved to Bari, a seaport town at the heel of southern Italy. The date of the transference of his grave is 1087 A.D., shortly before the Crusades. After the move, St. Nicholas became well known in western Europe. By that time, people were keeping careful records of dates and events. The moving of the grave was such an important occasion that the anniversary of its arrival in Bari is still celebrated there on May 8 each year.

The people of Bari recently expressed their continuing devotion to St. Nicholas when, on September 11, 2001, the small St. Nicholas church near the World Trade Towers in New York City was destroyed by falling debris. For the people of his city, the mayor of Bari sent a large monetary gift of half a million dollars to help restore this church—as did the people of Greece, who honor Nicholas as their nation's patron saint. People from many other countries and different denominations have also contributed to help rebuild the little church. Their devotion seems especially fitting because St. Nicholas is the patron saint of Manhattan, going back to the Dutch who were early settlers there. Interestingly enough, the name *Nicholas* is a very ancient word dating from the time of Homer and comes from the Greek meaning "victorious people."[1]

What strikes me as remarkable is that here we have a vital, vibrant, contemporary archetype so strong that sixteen hundred years after St. Nicholas's death, he is still a dearly beloved psychological and spiritual reality today! As Santa Claus, we've even moved him to the North Pole, right under the North Star—the most stable point in our heavens, often used by sailors to guide them. And yet, we have very few facts about Nicholas's actual life, because almost no written records were kept in the fourth century when he lived. In fact, Charles Jones, a recent professor at the University of California in Berkeley, tells us that not much was recorded about Nicholas until several centuries after his death. (Professor Jones worked for forty years to bring us what is now recognized as the leading scholarly book about St. Nicholas in English, *St. Nicholas of Myra, Bari, and Manhattan*.)[2] But we do have many legends

Statue of St. Nicholas in St. Nicholas's churchyard, Demre, Turkey

that go back to Nicholas's life in Myra, as Jones emphasizes. There are other important books on this subject, too, many in German. We are particularly grateful to Professor Felix Karlinger of the Universities in Salzburg and Munich, who went to eastern Europe and recorded many traditional folktales about St. Nicholas that I present to you in translation here (see bibliography). The information from these various sources paints a portrait of a living legend of a wise, grandfatherly, helpful, and generous man who makes our lives more meaningful through example. It is a legend that can balance the commercial, materialistic side of Christmas and have as much significance for us today as it did for people in the past.

In Myra, the traditional St. Nicholas Feast Day is still celebrated on December 6, which many believe to be the anniversary of St. Nicholas's death. This date is honored throughout Western Christendom, in lands comprising both Catholic and Protestant communities (in the Eastern Orthodox Church, the Saint's feast date is December 19). On December 5, the eve of St. Nicholas Day, some American boys and girls put their shoes outside their bedroom door and leave a small gift in hopes that St. Nicholas soon will be there. It was the early Dutch settlers who first brought this tradition to New York, which is how St. Nicholas became the patron saint of New York City.

Because St. Nicholas was the Bishop of Myra, statues, paintings, and stained-glass windows in different countries usually picture him carrying the traditional bishop's staff and wearing the customary hat or bishop's miter, as in the paintings you see in this book. Also, you will notice that he is slender. It was only in the early nineteenth century that Washington Irving first wrote about the generous gift giver as jovial and plump. Thomas Nast perpetuated this image in his many drawings and paintings used into the twentieth century.

In Switzerland, St. Nicholas is honored at the beginning of December around his feast day every year in many different forms. Near the woods around

Parade of men wearing colored, lighted St. Nicholas miters at night, Küssnacht on the Rigi Mountain, Switzerland

the city of Zürich, St. Nicholas has a small house where you can visit him, much as children in the United States visit Santa in department stores. Or St. Nicholas might visit your home. Different villages keep various traditions.

The Swiss mountain village of Küssnacht on the Rigi (mountain) holds very lively celebrations. The one I describe here is just one of many such events, but it is my favorite:

Out of the darkness, several hundred men wearing local traditional costumes appear, walking in step with large resounding cow bells around their waists. Left-right, left-right, in unison. The noise is very loud. Then comes another group of several hundred more men all wearing tall bishop's miters decorated like stained-glass windows and lit from within by candles.

These hats, about four feet high, commemorate St. Nicholas as a bishop whose miter was also rather high. The men of Küssnacht make the hats themselves using colored tissue paper with cardboard or lightweight wood. This custom of the candle-lit miters is rooted in a time long before the coming of electricity, when ancient people feared that the long cold nights of winter might last forever and the crops would never grow again. They lit big fires in the hope of magically helping to restore the strength of the sun. Today, when the men parade with traditional music through the village streets at night with their glowing, colorful miters, the effect is stunning. Perhaps some of you might want to make such a beautiful hat for yourselves.

These celebrations are now guided by local St. Nicholas societies and their members, both men and women, who keep the traditions alive. Besides organizing events such as parades and storytelling programs, they also send St. Nicholas representatives with small gifts and treats to people in hospitals and prisons and to the needy. These societies coach their members in the cultural history of St. Nicholas, so the conversations with them are more meaningful than that of simply telling Santa what you want for Christmas.

Early in December 2000, I had the opportunity to visit Prague. On St. Nicholas Eve, it seemed as if the whole city came out to greet the boys and men reenacting the ancient custom by dressing as the Saint. Everyone was very

friendly and cheerful in the plazas—refreshments were offered and there was a happy feeling in the air. This traditional celebration is so meaningful that it was continued even during the communist period before 1990. I was particularly interested to see children costumed as dark figures—such as devils—as well as angels! Some even wore horns on their heads lit by flashlights that could blink on and off. Light and then darkness; angels and devils. Somehow, St. Nicholas brings the opposites together in a playful and life-affirming way. In other cultures, this shadow side of St. Nicholas has other names and traditions. As we will read in "Anticipation," a memory of St. Nicholas Day by Anton Schnack, in Germany the companion's name is *Ruprecht*. In Switzerland, he is called *Schmutzli*. *Krumpus* is another German name for this companion figure.

I have also gone to Greece in search of St. Nicholas, and I have felt new life in my experience of him there. Every island seems to have its St. Nicholas chapel; every ship has its St. Nicholas icon. In my short visit, I met several people who have their own contemporary stories of St. Nicholas. Some of their stories appear in "Signs of St. Nicholas Today" at the end of the book.

Unlike a work of pure fiction, a legend always has some background in historical fact. Legends come from the oral tradition; that is, they are passed down from one generation to the next, often told by parents to their children. In this book, we start each section with one or more of these early legends about St. Nicholas. Then we present folktales that were still being told in the1950s in Europe, before television took the place of storytelling, along with some stories written by twentieth-century authors. To accompany the stories, we have brought together reproductions of paintings from the past that depict Nicholas in his formal, priestly role as well as later art showing the legendary Nicholas as the more playful, fun-loving, and down-to-earth figure whose spirit still pervades the early part of December in many eastern and western European countries.

Most of these stories and folktales appear here in English for the first time; although we have not changed the essential narrative in any of them, we have felt free to adapt and refine them for the modern reader. You will notice

that only one—"The Baker's Dozen"—is from America. The rest have a definite Old World tone. Somehow, and although the United States is famous as the "melting pot" of many cultures, the traditions of old St. Nicholas never really took hold here. My main purpose in presenting this book is to restore this rich heritage of the St. Nicholas of our ancestors to contemporary American people. You will also notice that many of the stories are not Christmas stories at all. Rather, for the most part they reflect the various roles St. Nicholas plays year-round as the patron saint of different aspects of life. We have presented these tales in all their diversity, sprinkled here and there with a few associated with the holidays. In particular, the first and last stories, "Anticipation" and "Holy Night," mirror the Christmas calendar and act as bookends for the tales that appear in between. (Incidentally, there are thirty-one stories in all—just enough for one each day in December!) Together, the collection tells one big story, mirroring what Gian Carlo Menotti, the great opera composer, recently described on National Public Radio as the four most important matters of the human spirit—love, compassion, outrage, and wonder.[3]

Even after so many centuries, St. Nicholas is more than a legend. And while slimmer than jolly old Santa, he is much more ample in character. The various stories and pictures we have gathered here help us find a larger-than-life St. Nicholas who is a healer, helper, and rescuer besides being a kindly, grandfatherly friend to children of all ages. As we have mentioned, St. Nicholas has long been known as the patron saint of sailors and others on their journeys. New Americans arriving by boat to our shores have often brought icons, or special pictures of St. Nicholas, to protect them from shipwreck. Likewise, this collection brings legends and stories from many countries that could help protect us from some of our own "shipwrecks" in life. We hope you will be inspired to read and tell these stories to one another again and again. We also hope they will help you find the generous spirit of the true St. Nicholas in your own hearts—on *any* day of the year.

ANTON SCHNACK

Anticipation—A Memory of St. Nicholas Day

EDITOR'S NOTE: *This memory of a small boy's* St. Nicholas Day, December 6, *in old* Germany *evokes the anticipation children feel everywhere for the wonderful gift bringer, but with some important differences from* American *children's experience of* Santa Claus: *In some countries,* St. Nicholas *had a companion with various names,* Ruprecht *being one of them, who asked the children questions about their behavior throughout the year. The treats and gifts* St. Nicholas *gave were often a reward for being "good."*

Oh, how I long to be a boy again, standing at the window at twilight with an ear pressed against the cold window pane, listening for every step stamping down the snow on our village street! The anticipation would take my breath away and make my heart pound. Dear, good St. Nicholas! Who could ever forget him? He made the long winter evenings short for boys and girls alike. With our childlike minds, we would gaze upward into the clear and shimmering night sky and imagine the bright stars to be his eyes. Eagerly we would search the heavens, hoping to catch a glimpse of St. Nicholas climbing down on a golden ladder carrying a heavy sack full of Christmas trees, dolls, shiny toy soldiers, chocolate figures, marzipan animals, juicy pears, cinnamon

Green-Robed Santa Claus, *German card, circa* 1900

cookies, nuts, and other wonderful treats—all for us! His appearance was like a dream we had had before and would dream again. Even into adulthood, it would leave traces of its sacredness and its wonder.

As my brother and sister and I anticipated St. Nicholas's coming, both song and prayer seemed to float down to earth and wander through the dark streets and sleeping gardens on soft soles, bringing joy, goodness, and love. We completely opened our hearts to this heavenly angel. Bewildered by our excitement, we would stumble over the recitation of our prayers, passionately promising always to obey our father and mother, never to lie, never to torment an animal, and always to think of God.

In those days, it seemed to us that the whole world was waiting for St. Nicholas! We would count the squares on the calendar until his feast day, December 6, and the hours, too. We could not wait until the preceding night—St. Nicholas Eve—when we would hang our stockings at the windows or put baskets in front of the door, hoping the generous Saint and his helper, Ruprecht, would fill them with candies and gifts.

The closer this magical time grew near, the more we felt the presence of the fantastic beings somewhere among us, larger than life. We would look around every corner in the corridor, behind every curtain that moved, behind every door to rooms we usually didn't enter. It took great courage to go out alone after dusk, and none of us dared to do it. As soon as it got dark, we would run home as fast as we could. Then, safe in our own living room, we would stare at the window until we thought we saw a giant shadow stride by, while we sat there with baited breath and inquisitive eyes.

One early December morning when I opened my school bag, out rolled three shining gold-paper-wrapped nuts! Hooray! That was the first sign! The next day, in the hoods and pockets of our coats we found more treats—spice cookies, little chocolate fish, coloring pencils—confirming our suspicion that St. Nicholas and Ruprecht were around.

That evening was the long-awaited St. Nicholas Eve. We placed the largest baskets we could find outside the door and went upstairs to prepare for bed.

Then suddenly, with an air of great importance, the grownups swept into our room. Ruprecht had just passed by, they whispered, and had thrown through the open window six beautiful apples. Here they were now! Our parents held the fruit high and distributed it with ceremony. Two were for my younger brother, John, two were for my older sister, Mary, and two were for me—Anton!

How fine the weight of those apples felt in my hands! Bright red on one side, golden yellow on the other, they were the most perfect apples I had ever seen. We thought they must have grown in some heavenly garden and been picked from trees where the distant silver stars glow. We were so moved by these mysterious, sacred apples that we set them on our bedside table and fell asleep gazing at them.

That night I dreamed of angels floating above my head while harp music rained blessings upon us. Long before dawn, I shook John and Mary awake and we all flew downstairs in our pajamas to see if St. Nicholas had come. . . .

Detail from Saint Nicholas with Scenes from His Life, *Russian, 16th century*

PART ONE

Gifts of Life and Freedom

The Legend of the Three Daughters

EDITOR'S NOTE: *Anton Schnack's story we've just read is full of memories about a magical being who brings marvelous gifts. The "Legend of the Three Daughters" is one of the first stories we have that portrays St. Nicholas in this way. It is the best known of all the legends and was apparently first recorded by Michael the Archemandrite. We've adapted this version from the account by Symeon as presented by Charles Jones. It has been dramatized many times.*

There was once a nobleman in Myra who had become so poor he could not even provide food for his three daughters. They would soon be old enough to marry. But the father could not hope to find husbands for them, for in those days a woman had to have a dowry to attract a husband.

In desperation, the poor man decided the only way to ensure the survival of his children was to sell them into servitude. At least that way they would have enough to eat, and perhaps he would be able to see them occasionally.

In due time, St. Nicholas heard of the father's sad plan. He felt he could not talk with the poor man face to face, but he thought and he thought until he found a secret way he could help.

The Charity of Saint Nicholas (*to the poor nobleman and his three daughters*) *by* Fra Angelico, 15*th century*

Late one night, Nicholas carefully wrapped something hard and heavy in a small leather bag. Then he waited until the moon was hidden by clouds. Quietly, quietly, he crept through the dark, empty streets until he came to the poor family's home. Inside, the three girls and their father were fast asleep. Stretching on tiptoe, St. Nicholas threw the heavy bag through the open window and then ran away as fast as he could.

In the morning, the poor father found the bundle on the floor. "It must be a prank," he thought, untying the thongs with cautious fingers. But when he opened it, he could not believe his eyes and began to weep for joy! There on his own floor, gleaming in the sunlight, was a large and precious pile of gold! But who could have brought it? The grateful father fell to his knees, thanking God for this generous gift. Soon afterward, his oldest daughter married a young gentleman from one of the region's best families, because now her father was able to provide a fine dowry for her, indeed.

But, alas, a year later the father was penniless again, about to sell his second daughter. Once more Nicholas went out in the black of night, completely unnoticed by anyone, and threw an equal amount of gold through the same window. Again in the morning the poor man couldn't believe his good fortune. But he remained dumbfounded. Where had the wonderful bags of gold come from? He wanted to know so that he could thank his benefactor. Reverently, he asked God to show him the angel who had made it possible for his two oldest daughters to marry. Then he lost no time in finding a good husband for the second one.

Over the next year, the poor man dared to hope that his third daughter could marry, too. He kept watching and waiting for the unknown servant of God. This time, he promised himself, he would find out who it was.

Eventually, the unknown servant of God *did* come again. But this time, the father was awake when the bag hit the floor—*Kachink*! As soon as he heard the sound of the gold, he leapt to his feet and ran even faster than Nicholas until he caught up with him. Immediately recognizing the Saint for who he was, the poor man dropped to his knees in thanksgiving, saying: "The good

Lord has awakened your pity. Without your help, I would have perished with my daughters!"

"I am glad to have been of service," Nicholas replied. "I only ask that you promise never to tell who has given you the gold."

EDITOR'S NOTE: *There ends the old legend. We imagine, though, that the grateful man agreed and was soon able to find a husband for his third daughter, too.*

As we have mentioned, St. Nicholas *is known as the patron saint of pawn brokers. The symbol for modern-day pawn brokers—three golden balls—is said to have come from this story. There are many pawn shops on* Lombard Streets *in both* London, England *and* Toronto, Canada. *You may find these balls in the windows there and in pawn brokers' windows all over the world, as I have in my own small town.*

PAUL KELLER

The Nicholas Ship

EDITOR'S NOTE: *Like* "Anticipation," *this is a vivid autobiographical memory of a boy's* St. Nicholas Day *in* Europe, *but with a significant difference:* Paul *remembers, not an abundance of gifts, but deprivation. In his boyhood struggle to accept reality, he learns that love and generosity are the greatest gifts of all.*

As St. Nicholas *was the patron saint of sailors, many real ships in* Europe *were named after him. Here the ship is a toy, but its* "St. Nicholas" *name is just as important in invoking a protective spirit.*

St. Nicholas never came to my house. But every year on December 5, he went next door to the rich family of Carl, the miller's son. The next day at school, Carl would always show me the wonderful gifts St. Nicholas had brought him. Yet I had received nothing. I couldn't understand why St. Nicholas never came to our house. I must admit I was really mad at him—even after my wise aunt tried to console me by saying, "Just look! Our house is so small. It could be that St. Nicholas has overlooked us accidentally. After all, he is an old man."

For a few years, I accepted this explanation; but when I was ten, I decided to wait outside and show St. Nicholas our little house myself. He always came

The Young Shipwright *by Robert Bruce Wallace*

at seven thirty, Carl had told me. So, at seven thirty on the evening of December 5, I was waiting on the street in front of the mill.

"St. Nicholas," I rehearsed, "please look; I live over there! In that little house just in back of the chestnut tree. If you go to the chestnut tree, you'll see our house for sure. I know my school lessons better than Carl, and I received a prize at the last school exam, and he didn't!"

That is what I wanted to say. I had thought it over for a long time and knew it by heart. Oh, but it was one of those fine speeches that was never to be spoken! When St. Nicholas really came—a tall man with a long, wild beard, a fancy belt, and a cap with a twisted tassel—I lost my courage and disappeared behind the picket fence, almost dying of excitement when I saw him go by. Only when he was quite far away did I get my courage back and called out for dear life:

"St. Nicholas! St. Nicholas! Wait! I live over there—in that little house! The one near the linden—no, the chestnut—tree. Near the CHE-SST-NNU-T TREE, St. Nicholas!"

But he didn't turn around. He disappeared as usual into the miller's house. I could see I wouldn't get any presents again that year! St. Nicholas had plugs in his ears. And besides, I had forgotten to mention the two most important things—my good grades and my school prize.

That night I lay wide awake in bed, unable to sleep. I knew I would never be happy again. Then, finally, came the great comforter—a dream that brought pure joy. I dreamed St. Nicholas gave me two beautiful presents, and they were just what I wanted.

The next day, once again Carl Miller brought his enormous pile of gifts from St. Nicholas to school. At first I wouldn't look at any of his things, but when he put a little wooden ship on the desk, I lost all self-control. It was a wonderful little boat with a mast and two cloth sails and even a little iron anchor. On the side of the boat, in cheerful, bright red letters, was painted the name: "St. Nicholas." It was just like a ship at sea.

I remember it all to this day. Suddenly I lay my head on my desk and began to cry as if my heart would break. At first the other children laughed at me, but then one ran to get the teacher, who was still drinking coffee in the teacher's lounge. Ours was a village school, and the lessons had not yet started.

I didn't tell the teacher why I was upset. But I did manage to stop crying and do my lessons. That day, I told Carl he couldn't copy my arithmetic. And when he got into trouble, I was happy. So what, he had a ship! If St. Nicholas had looked in the window, he would have seen his darling Carl Miller crouched over his desk, while I had all my problems solved!

Oh! Because of my hurt feelings, I was well on the way to becoming a very bad boy!

In spite of everything, Carl invited me to the creek that afternoon to play with his little boat; and I didn't even have a guilty conscience when I refused, saying, "No, no! Who would want to do anything so boring?"

Over the next two weeks, the teacher punished Carl several times for his poor work in arithmetic and in writing. I spitefully continued not to help him, but I can say without exaggeration that soon I was not so happy that he was getting into trouble.

Then on December 20, on our way home from school, Carl hurried up to me and pleaded, "Paul, *please* come over to sail my boat at the creek today!"

I can still see him begging me, and I remember how his brown eyes lit up his red, robust face. I hesitated for a moment, but my anger won out.

"You're just saying that because you want to copy my arithmetic tomorrow!"—and I turned my back on him.

That was really a cruel thing to say. I was very mean to Carl.

Later that day, I saw Mrs. Miller come screaming out of their yard, with Mr. Miller, too. . . . Later still, the strongest of their workers carried Carl out of the water. He had been playing with his toy boat and had fallen into the ice-cold mill creek.

They rushed Carl into the miller's house and the door slammed shut. Then everything was still and quiet, except for my pounding heart. I was really shocked and couldn't say a word. I just stood there, desperately wanting to know what would happen.

When it got dark and then darker and our streetlight was not lit, I became more worried and ran home. My grandfather and my aunt were sitting quietly in the parlor and did not speak when they saw me. And still the street lamps were not lit, so there was no light—no light! An evening storm came up suddenly, and I was afraid of storms in the dark. I crept to the fireplace for comfort, but our dog growled at me.

Suddenly a coach rumbled by, and we all hastened to the window. It was the miller's coach, swinging two glass lanterns.

"They are bringing the doctor," Grandfather observed.

"Who knows!" said my aunt.

I wanted to ask what she meant, but something stuck in my throat. What if Carl should die? My heart ached with fear. The possibility of Carl's death and my own feelings of guilt were so overwhelming I could hardly catch my breath. I *had* to know what was happening!

As soon as my grandfather and aunt left the room, I sneaked out and ran across the yard to the miller's house. I was afraid to ring the bell, so for a long while I waited, freezing at their front door. Finally, through the window I saw Marie, the maid, and tapped on the glass. When she came to the door, all she could tell me was that Carl was lying in bed with his eyes wide open, but he couldn't speak or hear. The doctor couldn't promise anything.

Slowly I turned around and left. For a long time I leaned on the miller's garden wall. Then I sat on our own doorstep and stared over at the lit windows of my sick friend's home. That was where my aunt found me when she took me inside and put me to bed.

I couldn't stop thinking about Carl. All that comforted me was that his eyes were open. Oh, if they would only stay open! I stretched my hands out on the covers and imagined I could hold Carl's eyelids open myself. Yes, I had to hold them open—I *had* to! If only I had gone with him that afternoon, he would not have fallen into the water. Now his eyes must not close. No, no, they must not! I held a piece of the cover between my thumb and middle finger as though it were Carl's eyelid.

Then, shamefully, I found myself thinking that if Carl died, we would have no school for a day and could sing that beautiful song, "Where is Home for the Soul?" Such thoughts made me shiver, and my thumb and middle finger pressed even tighter together.

All of a sudden I wanted to pray. With a frightened and humble heart, I began praying to St. Nicholas, the only saint with whom I was not on good terms. I even felt he had been right in not giving me a gift, because I was so naughty. But I hoped he'd have mercy on Carl. Surely he would; he had always been so good to Carl.

Three long days went by. I went to the well to wait for the neighbor's maid, Marie. She said that Carl's eyes were still open. If his eyes have been open for so long, he will surely get well, I thought. But I kept worrying that his eyes would close. And I could not understand why Carl couldn't see anything, even with his eyes open. I tried not to see with my eyes open, but I couldn't do it. Even at night, unless my eyes were firmly closed, I could see.

Finally, I asked my helpful and wise aunt for her opinion. She thought for a while and then said, "You know, Carl doesn't have a soul now." Why she should say that I don't know, but I believed her.

That was on December 23. It was fortunate that we were out of school for the holidays, because I couldn't have learned a thing or paid any attention. All I could think about was that Carl didn't have his soul.

Hour after hour I worried. Where could his soul have gone? It couldn't be in heaven, because Carl had not died. But if he didn't have it anymore, where *was* it?

That night, I lay awake for a long time. My heart beat loud and fast and my head was spinning. It felt so hot in my room!

Then all at once I bolted straight up in bed. I had figured it out!

When Carl fell into the water, his soul must have flown out of his mouth and into the creek. Carl's soul had *drowned*! Helplessly drowned! Oh, God! A boy's soul is so fine and delicate, like a thin, white shirt. And Carl's delicate soul had fallen into the icy mill creek where it must still lie, drowned and frozen.

The sweat was running off my face. Never since have I suffered such deep, hopeless feelings of fear and regret. For the first time in my young life, that night I was still awake when the clock struck midnight. Then in my utter exhaustion came a comforting thought:

The little boat! The little boat was also in the water. Maybe Carl's soul was in the boat!

The next morning—the day of Christmas Eve—I went to the well early and waited a long time until the miller's maid came.

"Are his eyes still open?" I asked anxiously.

"No, they have been closed since yesterday."

"Did he—has he—died?"

"No, he hasn't died yet."

She filled her jars with water and started home. I watched her go as if she were taking away my last hope. Carl had not died yet, Marie said, but he had already closed his eyes! This seemed to be a moment of the greatest danger. I *must* look for his soul—that is what mattered most!

In the chill late afternoon, I hurried out into the field to the mill creek about an acre away. My body shook in icy fear, but I went.

Along the creek I ran upstream. I longed to be on the other side, where the ground was firmer. Here, my feet were stuck in the mud holes.

Over there was the big old ash tree, jutting out over the water where it had fallen at an angle. Its gnarled arms waved eerily, filling me anew with fear. I half-turned to dash home, but then, as if in a dream, I saw Carl lying in front of me, eyes closed, crying loudly for help. I couldn't desert him! I ran, worried and afraid, to the ash tree and looked out over the creek. A mild frost covered the still surface of the water with a thin layer of ice. It looked like a shining mirror in front of me—like a smiling dead face!

Frozen! Now I wouldn't be able to find the boat. It would be stuck somewhere under the ice. Desperately, I searched slowly along the creek bank. Once I felt startled when I saw something white in the ice, but it was only an air bubble.

My head ached, and my feet slipped and slid on the frozen ground. A cuttingly cold wind was rising from the creek. What a sad walk for a boy on Christmas Eve!

Just when I was giving up hope, all at once I saw it! It seemed like a miracle!

Not far from shore, embedded in ice, there was Carl's little wooden ship. In the failing light, I could still make out the words *St. Nicholas* painted on its side, and I could see its little sails flapping in the wind.

I could also see that something white was in the ship. I stared, thinking at first it might be a dry leaf turned white by the hoar frost. But soon I realized it must be something much, much better. It was Carl's soul that was in the ship. Carl's little white soul was saved! Oh, hallelujah!

Sliding down on my knees to the edge of the creek, I grabbed a thin branch of the ash and bent far over the ice. I swung there for a moment between life and death and then caught the little boat in my free hand.

Once I had it, I didn't look at the boat again. No, I didn't dare; it was a sacred object. Like a priest carrying the holy chalice, I lifted the boat high and started back across the snowy field.

When the wind blew fiercely and the big, black birds flew screeching over my head, I pressed the little boat to my breast. Then the wind calmed, and the golden setting sun appeared from behind the clouds. Once again I lifted the little boat high in my hands. Walking slowly, happily, confidently, step by step I carried Carl's soul home.

My hand was stiff from the cold when I grabbed and pulled on the bell at the miller's door. The sound echoed through the house, bringing the miller himself in a flash. I spoke quietly and seriously, as if in prayer:

"I have Carl's ship! Look, his white soul is in it!"

The miller stared at me, and I looked back at him in complete faith. Without speaking, he gently took the little boat and carried it into the house. Then I went home.

Later that evening, before we had lit the lights of our Christmas tree, our own bell rang. Opening the door, I was surprised to see the miller. He apologized

for coming but said he wanted to share his happy news with us because we had asked about Carl so often. The doctor had just declared that Carl was now definitely going to get well again.

My grandfather and my aunt gathered around the miller. But I couldn't move and didn't say a word. Even when the miller told us the details, I was silent, as if in prayer.

But I was listening intently, and I could hardly contain my joy as Carl's father reported: "When your son Paul pulled our bell so hard, Carl woke up at last out of his deep sleep. We all looked at him in wonder. It was so odd that he became conscious again just at the moment when Paul believed he had brought Carl's soul back in the little St. Nicholas ship."

FRENCH FOLKTALE

St. Nicholas Buys a Young Man His Freedom

EDITOR'S NOTE: *The French are famous for their feeling for* eros*—or romance. As the patron saint of couples,* St. Nicholas *enters into this spirit, too.*

There was once a widow who had only one son. Because she wanted him to go into his father's business, she gave him all the money she had—seventy coins of gold.

"Take these!" she said to the boy. "Go to sea and buy spices and other fine things that we can sell at a handsome profit here at home!"

The young man took the seventy gold coins, bade his mother farewell, and set off to board the ship he hoped would take him to find his fortune. On the way, he entered a church whose patron was St. Nicholas. While he was praying, he heard a voice sigh behind him: "Alas, my church is falling to pieces because no one will contribute to its repair."

Startled, the young man looked around the sanctuary, but he didn't see anyone in the dim light. As soon as he resumed his prayers, though, he heard the voice again:

Saint Nicolas, *detail of stained glass, 13th century,* Chartres Cathedral, Chartres, France

"Oh! If only a good man would take care of my church, it could be saved from ruin. I would be so grateful!"

Once more the young man looked around but saw no one. Then, just as he was about to cross himself and leave, he heard the voice for the third time: "If only my church could be restored, how happy I would be!"

The young man rose quickly from his knees and searched everywhere, but there was still no one to be found. Bewildered, he went to the church priest and told him what had happened.

"Yes, it is true," the priest replied. "Our church is in sore need of repair."

"And what would it cost?"

"That's the problem! We need at least sixty pieces of gold, and I don't have even one. Most of the people in my congregation are poor—and the few others are stingy."

Reconsidering his own plans, the young man thought to himself: "I have seventy gold pieces. If I give sixty, I'll still have ten left for my business."

Without delay, he handed sixty gold coins to the astonished priest. Then he boarded ship and sailed away.

At first, all went well. The young man traveled all the way to the Orient, where he bought fine spices and perfumed oils and exquisite silk cloth. Then he packed his rich merchandise and boarded another ship bound for home.

But the ship soon fell into the hands of some wicked pirates. After stealing from the passengers everything they had, the scoundrels put them in chains and dragged them to the slave market to be sold—including our young man!

In that way the young man came to be bought by a rich *pasha*— a man of high-ranking office in Turkey.

This pasha had in his harem many wives and countless daughters—among them one who was particularly beautiful and known throughout the land for her breathtaking ability to dance. One evening, the pasha commanded this daughter to perform. She did, her body swaying gracefully to the flowing rhythms of the flute. While serving his master, the young man saw the girl dancing and was instantly struck by her beauty.

Soon afterward, this daughter noticed the young man working in the garden. Something about him caught her eye, too, and somehow she found a way to approach and speak to him.

Who knows? Perhaps she asked for a drink of water from his pouch, and when he gave it to her, their eyes met and lingered. Perhaps it was the birdsong or the sweet scent of jasmine in the air. Or perhaps it was the purity of their hearts. Whatever the reason, the young man and the girl began to meet secretly and soon fell in love.

But their love appeared hopeless: He was a slave without freedom or property, and she was the daughter of a mistrusting and jealous pasha.

One evening the young man prayed to St. Nicholas in desperation, saying, "I helped you, dear Saint. Won't you now please help me?"

"Yes, my son," he heard a voice answer. "Indeed I will, God willing!"

The very next day a stately older gentleman rode up to the pasha's palace. When he was led to the pasha, he said, "I saw a slave on your grounds I liked—a young man who works in the garden. I would like to buy him. How much does he cost?"

The pasha answered, "Ten pieces of gold."

"He is not worth that much! You bought him yourself for only three."

"How do you know that?"

"Oh, I have my sources! I offer you five pieces, and that is too much."

But the pasha was a hard businessman, so at last they agreed on seven pieces of gold.

That very day the stately older gentleman rode away with the young man, who was happy to be free, but sad to leave the girl.

"What's the matter, my generous friend?" asked the older man, who was, of course, St. Nicholas. When the young man shyly told him, he nodded. "I see how it is," he said, eyes twinkling. "I will also have to buy your sweetheart from that old miser!"

Back to the palace the stately older gentleman rode alone. Once more he met with the pasha, pretending that he wanted to buy the girl for his own harem.

The pasha was a shrewd bargainer; who knows how much St. Nicholas had to pay! Whatever the price, it wasn't long before he led the girl away to the waiting young man, who greeted them both with tears of joy.

St. Nicholas told the happy couple, "I have a ship lying in the harbor. I'll tell the captain he should take you to France. Don't worry, the ship is very fast and will outrun all pirates. And here is some merchandise. You paid sixty gold pieces for me," he said to the young man, "and now you will have goods of equal value for yourself."

And so the couple sailed to France, where they soon married with the blessing of the young man's mother.

Some say that the young man and his wife cared well for his mother and that she led a good, long life. Some say that St. Nicholas came to their wedding. Who knows? One is more likely to hear him than see him. Perhaps St. Nicholas was there, perhaps not. But the people who *were* there say the wine and honey that flowed on that day was beyond compare. *Mon Dieu*! We may never taste wine like that again in this world!

ROMANIAN FOLKTALE

The Moneybag of Molsch Talpasch

EDITOR'S NOTE: *This story reminds us that St. Nicholas was the patron saint of businessmen. Curiously, while a folktale, it is nevertheless told in the first person. While contrary to convention, that is how it comes to us.*

When I was a small boy and my grandfather very old, we would sit together by the fire on long winter evenings, and he would tell me stories about his life and the people he had known.

One of them was a man called Molsch Talpasch, a salesman who traveled all around the countryside with his horse and wagon showing his wares. He was hardworking enough, Grandfather said, but quite an ordinary fellow—not too good, not too bad—a man like you or me. I remember looking at my grandfather in the flickering light—his gentle hands at peace in his lap, his white beard resting on his chest—and thinking there was nothing ordinary about *him* at all. But his voice had dropped, and I didn't want to miss a word, and so I settled in closer and listened.

One evening, Molsch was out on the road rather late—I don't remember if my grandfather said where; perhaps it was near the Moldau River. He stopped at an inn for some warmth and supper. After serving him a meal of thick stew

and dark bread, the innkeeper's wife said, "Stay here tonight! Why go any further? It will be dark in an hour, and then you would not want the company of anyone you might meet." She meant that there were many bandits about, as was true in those days. Some people had even lost their lives.

But Molsch just laughed and shook his head. "Thank you kindly, but no. Tomorrow I must be in this town and that village, and the day after, I am expected somewhere else."

The innkeeper's wife shrugged at his foolishness until she saw the coins he pulled from a large leather bag and left on the table. Then she frowned at losing the opportunity to lodge such a wealthy customer. But what could she do but say "Very well!" and let him go?

And so Molsch Talpasch hitched up his horse and wagon and set forth into the lengthening shadows. The late autumn air was sharp, but the evening sky was clear and promised starlight. All was well until the road turned into the woods. The horse, with a sense beyond his master's, slowed down in the closing darkness, and the wagon wheels creaked and squeaked as they road over the bumpy tree roots.

Molsch hadn't gone far when he thought his tired eyes must be playing tricks, for it seemed in the gloom that the trees ahead were moving.

Then suddenly, as if from nowhere, he was surrounded by a group of men.

"Give us your money, or you're dead!" they shouted.

Something heavy struck Molsch on the back of his head. He heard his horse whinny frantically as he fell off the wagon seat. Then he knew nothing.

When he regained consciousness, his first thought was that it was odd to be lying on the ground. Where was the wagon? Where was his horse? Why was it so cold? He realized he was wearing only his shirt and shorts—his coat, trousers, and boots were gone. And his face was wet and sticky to the touch with blood. He was on his stomach in the dirt. With great effort, he tried to stand, but couldn't. His whole body trembled.

"St. Nicholas, help me!" he stammered, praying over and over again to the guardian of his childhood.

Moments later, as if in a dream, he felt the presence of someone bending over him. In the darkness he could not see who it was, but he was aware that he suddenly felt relieved. It seemed he was being lifted up onto a donkey. He felt the warmth of a blanket fall over his legs and shoulders and the support of a firm hand at his back so that he would not fall. Then he lost consciousness again and knew nothing.

When he woke up, his bones ached and his head throbbed . . . but he was lying in a bed! A fine, soft bed, with sweet smelling linens and feather pillows. He tried to call out, making a croaking sound. In response, the door swung open, and there stood the innkeeper's wife.

"Look what happened to you!" she clucked. "To be sure, it's not for me to remind you, sir, but you should have stayed here!"

"Who brought me?"

"An old man. I forget his name, if he gave it. He had a white beard and was well dressed. A rich man, I don't doubt."

"I offered him our finest room," she went on, "warning him that if he went back out into the night, things could go wrong for him, too. But the old man just chuckled and said, 'Nothing will happen to me. But see here! This is the moneybag of Molsch Talpasch. The bandits must have lost it in the woods. Please see that it is returned to him safely. And watch for his horse—it will come back sometime today, ready for a full bucket of oats! Only the wagon is kaput. No matter; it was already a wreck.'"

"You're sure he didn't say his name?" Molsch pressed. "Could it have been—*Nicholas*?"

"I don't rightly remember," the innkeeper's wife answered. "But he was a fine gentleman; any one could see that. I brought out a bottle of our best wine, hoping he would stay the night. But he just said I should give it to you—and take good care of you, too. Then he left. He called you his friend, sir. Don't you know who it was?"

Molsch Talpasch wanted to nod his head, but it ached too much. Seeing him in pain, the innkeeper's wife lay the heavy moneybag at his side and

quietly left the room, anticipating the fine tip she was sure to receive.

Later that day, Molsch's horse did come back—who knows from where? The innkeeper's wife fed the animal a full bucket of oats, just as the stranger had suggested. And when Molsch felt fit enough to be on his way again, the gold coins he left on the table surpassed all the good woman's hopes.

And so my grandfather would always end the story. "But *was* it St. Nicholas?" I would plead to know. Grandfather would never say, but his eyes would crinkle with the merriment of the fine old gentleman himself when he answered, "What do *you* think?"

ADOLF LEOPOLD

The Russian Icon

EDITOR'S NOTE: *This story from* World War II *could have occurred in a remote* Russian *village in the no-man's land between the* Russians *and the* Germans. *As we know from myths and folklore, thresholds are often places where miraculous events occur.*

After hours of being on the road, the army lieutenant and his driver can finally see by the light of the colorful dawn that it is going to be a beautiful winter morning. Everywhere the birch trees sparkle in the radiant sunshine. Even the telephone lines look festive, swooping gracefully from pole to pole like hoarfrost garlands. The day has become clear and bright by the time the two men in their car come to where the road to the village they are looking for seems to turn off the main route; at least, that's what an old sign indicates. The distance is apparently only about six more kilometers, but the road gets worse and worse. Ahead, they can see that wood has been taken out of the forest; perhaps loggers' trucks are responsible for the sharp ruts in the road.

The men drive to the edge of the forest but can go no further in the deep snow. They lock the car and camouflage it with a few branches, leaving their steel helmets inside—fur caps are much better at thirty-five degrees below zero. Then they trudge into the woods on foot.

Detail from Saint Nicholas with Scenes from His Life, *Russian, 16th century*

In the lieutenant's lunch box is a package from home. He wants to wait until he's on his way back to open it. He imagines it as his reward if everything goes well on this assignment.

They can only move slowly; the forest seems to have no end. It is early afternoon before they come, at last, to an opening in the birch woods, where they see a small house some distance away.

The sight of the simple dwelling with smoke rising from its chimney encourages the tired men. They try to quicken their steps through the heavy snow; then they knock and open the door without waiting to be invited. Framed in the winter light, the lieutenant greets everyone inside in stumbling Russian: "*Dobree den* (Good day)! *Vashe derevnya, kak nazivayctsa* (What is the name of your village)?"

Shocked, a young mother rises from the tile bench where she has been sitting and answers, "*Grasnaya! Gerodnya!*"

"*Vielen dank, geehrte frau* (Many thanks, dear madam)!" the nervous lieutenant inadvertently responds in German—for indeed, he and his driver are of that nationality.

When the two German soldiers become accustomed to the relative darkness of the living room, they notice the grandparents sitting near the tile stove and do their best to ignore the scowl on the grandfather's face. Then they see the three children lying on a board stretched across two stones. The next moment, they become keenly aware of something else: Suddenly from behind the stove rise three men, their bodies looming large in the small room. After only a cursory glance at the Germans, they leave quickly without saying anything.

Both of the travelers realize that these men must be partisans hiding in this Russian home. They won't want to miss the opportunity to kill two Germans. They may have hidden weapons and be waiting outside. Or perhaps they will alarm companions who are also waiting to spring a trap.

The Germans stiffen. What should they do? How can they get help? Should they leave the house? Should they leave the village and try to reach the forest? But they have not yet finished their assignment. It is doubtful that they could make it back to the forest without being killed. Both men are exhausted. Silently, they read the message in each other's eyes: We're trapped; we aren't going to get out of here alive.

They have to do something, and quickly, but what? To the driver's amazement, the lieutenant then acts in a way that seems completely inappropriate to their dangerous situation. In the room where they stand, five or six sacred pictures hang in a row on the wall. The lieutenant looks at them in meditation, as is his habit wherever he finds such icons. On one, he sees the old Russian script and says the name aloud in the troubled silence: "Nicholas."

The grandfather, who had had such a dark look when the Germans first entered, is the first to speak: "*Da, da, Nikolai dobree, Nikolai kharasho* (Yes, yes, good Nicholas, fine Nicholas)!" The lieutenant repeats, "*Nikolai dobree, Nikolai karasho*," and expresses his pleasure at finding this picture of St. Nicholas on the wall.

With those words, the strained atmosphere is broken. The old man nods to Matka, the young mother, who immediately leaves the room. The Germans can hear whispering outside. What is being discussed—life, or death?

After a while, the door opens and Matka returns with a bundle of straw that she spreads on the floor. Her gesture means: You may sleep here.

But what transpired outside, the Germans don't know. Do they dare accept the invitation, or is it only a trap? Who can say! Outside, it is beginning to get dark, and the lieutenant thinks, "I must look the village over to decide if it is suitable for headquarters. But there is no sense in going out at nightfall. That would only bring out the partisans."

"*Spasiba* (thanks), Matka!" he says. Then he and his driver say goodnight to the family and lie down wearily on the floor. They are soon aware that the rest of the household has gone to sleep except for the watchful grandfather, still sitting silently by the tile stove.

"Good night, William," the lieutenant says simply to his driver. "We'll see tomorrow what it is that God wants."

Eyes closed, he folds his hands in prayer and these words of an old evening song come to him:

Let the angel of protection
Come to keep us from deception
So we sleep in peace in Thy name.
With the angels of the Holy Trinity
We praise Thee in eternity.
Amen.

Exhausted, the two German soldiers quickly fall asleep. They couldn't have stayed awake to keep watch, and it wouldn't have helped them, anyway.

When they awaken, the bright winter sun is already shining through the low windows of the living room. The light strikes the wall just under the icon of St. Nicholas, whose day it is today—December 6! All night long, the front door has been left unlocked, presumably so that the partisans could have returned at will, if necessary. Just across from it is the small low bench where the grandfather is sitting with a big smile. He has kept watch on his guests the whole night, in part because he knows they are probably enemies of his motherland, Russia, but in part because he also knows they love St. Nicholas.

The lieutenant takes his daily prayer book out of his knapsack and reads the entry for the sixth of December, 1941: "When Jacob awoke from his sleep, he said, 'Certainly the Lord is at this place, and I did not know it.'"

Something about this passage inspires the lieutenant to wait no longer to open his package from home. On the top he finds a small photograph of his four children and a card they wrote him, and on the card is a picture of St. Nicholas reproduced from an old painting. Heart full of love for his family, the lieutenant gazes at the photograph and then at the picture, involuntarily murmuring, "Nicholas!"

Matka has been standing next to him as he sits on the floor. Hearing him, she points over his shoulder to the icon on the wall and then back again to the picture on the card, saying, "*Nash Nikolai, vash Nikolai* (Our Nicholas,

your Nicholas)." She lets her children climb off the tile stove bench to look at the picture of St. Nicholas, and she also allows them to taste the homemade cookies the strangers have brought from a far-away place that they have never seen. It is St. Nicholas Day, after all!

But now the time has come to part. As a token of his thanks for her friendly hospitality, the lieutenant gives the young mother the card with the picture of St. Nicholas. At first she doesn't want to accept it, but then she goes to the corner of the room where she keeps her icons. Her eyes linger on a colorful picture of the Virgin Mary from which she cannot bear to separate. Hesitating only briefly, she removes it from the wall and offers it to the lieutenant.

But in the meantime, the lieutenant has found a small, dark picture of Jesus Christ, blackened with age. It is painted on wood and already has lots of wormholes. The lieutenant asks the young mother for this picture instead, and she nods shyly, relieved that she can keep her beloved image of the Virgin. Kissing the Christ icon, she offers it with a gracious bow to her guest.

Now the German driver has something to offer, too. He gives Matka a glass of honey he has received from home and a highly prized bottle of salt, as well. Her eyes shine with pleasure at these treasures. Then at the front door, the grandparents and Matka embrace the strangers and offer their hand: "*Dosvidanya* (Good-bye)!"

That day, the two Germans soon finish their investigation of the village, easily determining that the houses will make adequate facilities for the doctors to care for wounded soldiers. As the lieutenant and his driver return, they walk by the hospitable home once again. Matka stands at the door, waving for them to come in.

She shows them the wall where both Nicholas icons are now hanging next to each other and softly calls out, "*Nash Nikolai, vash Nikolai* (Our Nicholas, your Nicholas)!"

The lieutenant pulls out his worm-eaten wooden picture and says, "*Nash Khristos, vash Khristos, aden*" (one Christ). Kneeling over the icon, the grandfather makes the sign of the cross over his guests. Wide-eyed, the three children stare in astonishment at the grownups, realizing that something great has happened here—something having to do, not with the war, but with peace.

Soon afterward, the new friends say good-bye for the last time, with much shaking of hands and kissing of cheeks. Then the Russians all stand in the door watching the strangers in their fur caps as they plod their way towards the nearby birch forest with its hoarfrosted branches.

✠ ✠ ✠

The two German soldiers and the Russian family never saw one another again. Many years later, one of those German men is now buried on foreign soil. The other remembers that they spent St. Nicholas Day, December 6, 1941, in a friendly home far away in what was then the Soviet Union. His worm-eaten wooden icon of Blessed Christ the King hangs in a place of honor in his home. We do not know what happened to the Russian family, but we join the German lieutenant in sending a prayer for their well-being.

LUDWIG SCHUSTER

St. Nicholas Brings It to Light

EDITOR'S NOTE: *In this story,* St. Nicholas *acts through a village shepherd who has dressed to play the part for the annual* St. Nicholas Day *celebration.* As *we also see in* "The Legend of the Three Stratilates," *from the very earliest times* Nicholas *was known for protecting prisoners.* This *concern will come as no surprise when we learn that* Nicholas *himself was probably imprisoned during the reign of* Diocletian*—the* Roman *emperor who preceded* Constantine*—simply because* Nicholas *was a* Christian. When Constantine *became the first* Christian *emperor, he freed those whom* Diocletian *had so persecuted, including* Nicholas.

A November fog blankets the valley. The moon casts a milky shadow over the farmhouses while the village sleeps, protected by the thick fog. A single beam of light shines out of an open window on the empty streets. As if in a dream, a chain rattles in a barn, and in the distance a dog barks. The clock on the tower strikes like a great, heavy gong, and then all is quiet near and far. Midnight approaches with its silence, its peace.

But under a certain roof on the outskirts of the village, all is not quiet. There something spits and crackles! Hissing maliciously, it spreads unattended and unseen—fire!

Straw burns easily; the hay is dry and wants to burn, too. The hot flames grow, leaping upward until they cannot be contained, and a high, bright blaze

spirals upward and bursts through the shingles of the barn, shattering the quiet with a huge roar.

"Fire! Fire at the Leitner farm!" From house to house, the cry for help echoes through the night. People wake up in alarm. Lamps are lit; doors fly open. The fire fighters grab their helmets and their hoses, and the fire truck begins to roll, its horn blaring amidst the shouting of orders. Volunteer helpers and concerned neighbors gather at the burning barn, now all lit up with red and yellow flickering beams and restless shadows.

"Fire!" The church bells clang in the tower and a sweet sticky smell hangs like a cloud in the damp air. "Fire! The barn is burning at the Leitner farm!" Everyone is awake by now, and the quiet night has become like a frightening, busy day, full of excitement, noise, and hurry.

Throughout the night, the villagers pour water onto the charcoal beams. At the pale sunrise, all that remains of the Leitner barn is a smoking pile of ruins. The family's home itself is saved, but the barn with their entire harvest has been destroyed.

The farmer Matthew Leitner stares at the disaster, hardly able to believe it. His large hands, usually so capable, hang useless at his sides. Here, now, there is nothing he can do. . . .

Meanwhile, the fire commissioner is energetically at work. After his phone call, the police captain has arrived, and they are deeply engaged in conversation. It seems that recently, there have been a number of cases where people have burned down their own buildings just to get the insurance money.

The two men investigate the scene. Then the policeman approaches Farmer Leitner, still standing immobilized at the sight of his destroyed property.

"Are you insured?" inquires the policeman.

"Yes," the farmer answers, "up to eight thousand."

The other men nod in silence and continue to rummage around. What might they find under the soaked, black hay and straw?

Then suddenly, they do find something—something suspicious and very incriminating. It is a can, a blue metal can with a handle and a spout. It is

badly scorched, but on its side the black stenciled letters can still be clearly read: *Kerosene*!

The Leitners are highly respected in the village, so the policeman is very polite as he asks the farmer's wife, Anna, if she recognizes this can. Indeed she does—in spite of its altered appearance. It is, in fact, her own gas can, but how in the world did it get here? Dumbfounded, she has no explanation.

But exchanging glances, the two officials do. "This is the end of our work here," says the police captain. The fire commissioner nods and carries the gas can to his car.

The policeman walks up to the farmer with some reluctance. The task he must perform is an unpleasant one, for he knows Matthew Leitner well. They have eaten together, and he has always considered the farmer to be a well-mannered and industrious man. Leitner has sold him fruit trees and bees. And now this. But it has to be done; there is no way around it. It is his duty.

"Matthew, I am sorry, but we must"—he averts his eyes from the farmer's confused expression—"we have to take you with us."

"But why?"

"Just come along, everything will be explained."

Still not comprehending, the farmer obediently follows the policeman to the waiting car.

"What's this about, Matthew?" his wife insists, rushing to his side. "What's going on?"

She would have pressed him further, but at that very moment a child's voice calls in alarm, "Mama!" It is little Barbara, the Leitners' four-year-old daughter, standing at the front door in her nightgown. She must have slept through all the excitement and know nothing about the fire. Now she's looking anxiously for her mother, who is usually at her bedside when she awakens.

The farmer's wife runs to the child and warms her bare feet with her hands. She wants desperately to speak with her husband—and to look into his eyes to see what they would say. But when she turns around, she sees that the policemen have already left, taking him along.

Not everyone is gone, though. Many of the villagers are still standing around, looking at Anna in a strange way. "Humph," they seem to be saying, "That Leitner appeared to be a good man, but now we see what he really is—an arsonist! Farmer Leitner's an *arsonist*!"

After these events, all was quiet around the old barn. The fire engine was gone, and only two guards remained to keep watch over the smoldering ruins. Now back in their homes, the villagers who had witnessed Leitner's arrest kept thinking, "So that's it—he's an arsonist!" It didn't take long for the gossip to go around town.

The next day the prison pastor visited Farmer Leitner in jail, leaving him a book of legends about St. Nicholas of Myra.

After the pastor left, Leitner opened the book to a legend he had been reading at home, before his disaster: " As early as the fourth century A.D. in Asia Minor (now Turkey), prisons already existed, and some of the prisoners in them were innocent. The Bishop—later called 'Saint'— Nicholas once freed such an innocent man. His kind action took place many centuries ago and far away. But for God and His Saints there is no time and place, and the human heart is always the same."

When the farmer read these words, his own heart filled with hope, and he prayed to God for help. He also prayed to Nicholas, grateful in advance for the Saint's intercession he trusted would come: "As we give our children apples and nuts in memory of you, please also give this gift to me—God willing, may my innocence be proven so that I may go home to my work and to my wife and our little Barbara."

As he thought of his daughter, tears came to his eyes. Who knew when he would see her again? He only knew he wouldn't be there for St. Nicholas Day this year. Last year, Barbara had been so loveable when she had run to him in the presence of the man with the long white beard and his sack over his shoulder. How sweetly she had folded her hands as she stumbled over the Lord's

Prayer. She couldn't say it correctly, but one could tell by her tone of voice that she felt it was holy—

Leitner's memories were interrupted when the guard entered his cell to put down the bed for the night. As he lay down, the farmer thought, "Now little Barb is going to bed, too." He imagined how she snuggled in her pillows, hugging her beloved doll, Nanni. . . .

But that's not how things were at the Leitner farm. The farmer's daughter Barbara was not putting her doll to bed, for Nanni could not be found. Her mother had looked for the doll everywhere, but no one had seen it since the night of the fire.

Whenever Anna spoke of the doll, Barbara would only shake her blonde hair and repeat, "Nanni not here! Nanni not here!"

In time, the doll was forgotten and the child turned to other things. Her mother had much weightier topics to think about: Anna Leitner had been ordered to appear in court as witness against her husband. On December 15, she would have to say that it was her own kerosene can they had found on the site of the fire. It was this incriminating evidence that had put her husband in jail. But how could she say anything else? The truth is the truth, even if it is a matter of life and death. After all, no one can be saved with a lie. . . .

On the evening of December 5, all at once mother and daughter heard someone outside their home, rattling the latch at the gate. Who could it be?

"Pay attention, Barb," said Mrs. Leitner. "He's coming now, our holy Bishop St. Nicholas! No, you needn't be afraid. I'm sure he is going to bring you something good. Just recite your Lord's Prayer for him. You can do it!"

Just then the doorbell rang, and Anna opened the door to admit the tall, white-bearded man. Little Barbara pressed herself in the corner near the tile stove and looked at him expectantly, happy and afraid at the same time. She didn't know their visitor was actually Mr. Silcher, the shepherd, dressed up as the Bishop for the village children's celebration of St. Nicholas Day. She almost had to laugh, for the door was low and the Bishop's hat was very high. It almost tumbled off!

The prosecutors could take the view that the child had been talked into the story about the doll and making a fire in the barn. A small child can easily be influenced to believe what she has been told."

Silcher looked at him in horror.

"I believe your story," the mayor assured him, "but I am afraid the officials might not believe it. Naturally, I will not express any of my doubts in my report for tomorrow."

Somewhat satisfied, the shepherd returned to the Leitner farm to retrieve his sack and Bishop's hat. Patting his beard back into place, he then continued his rounds to the children of the village. In every home, he repeated the story of what had taken place at the Leitner farm. By the next day, everyone in town knew about it.

Leo Anselm and Gary Balthes found out in another way. They were the men who were doing the cleanup work at the Leitner barn. It was their job to shovel the rubble from the walls and the burnt hay onto a truck to be hauled away. On the day after little Barbara's confession, suddenly something caught Anselm's eye. He put his shovel aside, bent over, pushed the sand and rubbish away, and picked up something hard and glossy.

"What is this?" He turned the thing around and showed it to Balthes, who, curious, came closer. Then Balthes recognized the object for what it was.

"They are eyes," he cried out in surprise. "Shiny doll's eyes! See this wire at the back? That's where they were attached to the head. I am sure of it. Last week my daughter Stephanie broke her doll's head, and the eyes looked just like these. And here, look!" He pointed down and bent over. "Here are some pieces of pink porcelain."

The two men picked up the pieces and examined them carefully. They could recognize a doll's mouth, ear, nose, and eyebrows, as well as the forehead where the blonde hair had been. The pieces were dark brown where the glue had discolored in the heat of the fire.

Right away, the two men took their findings to the city hall and testified to the truth of their statements. The mayor was very, very pleased. He wrapped

the small but critical bits of proof with the shepherd's report and mailed the package that same day. This evidence would be sufficient to restore Matthew Leitner's freedom and honor.

A few days later, the prison pastor shook the hand of the former prisoner with heartfelt joy in his eyes, saying, "You see, Matthew, our holy Bishop Nicholas can and does want to help us. He *has* helped, as we now see! It was not in vain that you believed in him during your troubles."

The pastor went on: "Some people might say it was just a coincidence that you read about Nicholas freeing innocent prisoners and prayed to him, or that your daughter told her story to Silcher dressed as the Bishop. But I believe that our dear Saint himself stepped in quietly to help you. Even the real Nicholas of old did not want to be recognized when he did something good. We know, for instance, of how he helped a poor man's daughters by throwing bags of gold through the window and then disappeared into the night because he didn't want to be seen or thanked."

"But I *do* thank him today, and I *will* thank him every day for the rest of my life," said Leitner, his voice trembling with joy and gratitude.

Upon his release, the first thing Matthew Leitner did was to buy a new doll. Then the farmer with the large, capable hands went home to his waiting family and began to build a new barn.

Detail from Saint Nicholas with Scenes from His Life, *Russian, 16th century*

PART TWO

A Friend for the Journey

The Legend of the Three Stratilates

EDITOR'S NOTE: *Like the earlier story,* "St. Nicholas Brings It to Light," *this one presents* Nicholas *as the patron saint of prisoners.* As *early as the sixth century, the legend of the three* stratilates (*military officers*) *appeared in written form in* Latin *and attracted the attention of the Church. According to author and scholar* Charles Jones, *it is, in fact, the first legend that prompted the* Church *to take special notice of* Nicholas. *Previously,* Nicholas *was regarded not as a saint, but merely as a* Myran *bishop who came to have a very good reputation among the local inhabitants. One of the earliest versions of the legend can be retold this way:*

One day, the Roman emperor Constantine sent three commanding officers with a contingent of troops to sail from their headquarters in Constantinople to a distant province. On their way, the wind became too calm to sail any further, so they stopped at Andriake, the port of Myra. A few of the sailors who went into town soon found themselves accused of looting—but in truth, they were innocent! The real thieves had set them up so that the townsfolk would blame the visiting soldiers for the thieves' own crimes.

Before long, a crowd had surrounded the suspects and begun to riot. The noise grew so loud that Nicholas, all the way from his home in nearby Myra,

Saint Nicholas of Bari Liberating Three Innocent Prisoners *by Fra Angelico, 15th century*

heard the hubbub. He quickly walked to the port where the commotion was, intending to investigate and restore peace.

When he arrived, the three officers and some of their men explained what had happened. Together, they managed to quiet the crowd. Then Nicholas invited the visitors to be guests in his home. But on their way, some of the townsfolk reported that three of the innocent sailors had been taken into custody. What's more, they had already been sentenced to death! Since Nicholas was so much respected in the area, they trusted he would somehow be able to save the men.

Nicholas and the ship's officers ran immediately to the place where the execution was to be held. There they saw that the hands of the three accused men were bound behind them and that their faces were covered. They were about to be beheaded! They were kneeling, heads bent down, expecting death at any moment. The executioner had already positioned his sword over the first victim. (In all due respect, it is important to add that this grim reaper had been stalling, though—hoping that Nicholas might appear before he had to perform his horrible duty.)

Nicholas fearlessly grabbed the executioner's sword and threw it to the ground. Untying the three men, he escorted them away from the crowd until he was sure they were safe. Then he walked over to the local magistrate's office. "How could you have allowed such a miscarriage of justice to occur in your district?" Nicholas reproached him. But the dishonest magistrate tried to pass the blame on to other officials, retorting, "I had nothing to do with the whole bloody affair!"

Nicholas, however, knew better. He had previously learned that the magistrate had accepted a large bribe for letting the unjust sentence stand, even though he knew this action amounted to cold-blooded murder. Furious, Nicholas would have punished the dishonest magistrate; but the ship's officers—who were very kindhearted men—persuaded him to pardon the man, after all.

At last the ship, with its three officers and all their original crew, once again set sail, eventually returning to Constantinople. When the people learned

of the officers' generosity and the whole venture, they welcomed them as heroes and gave them a great homecoming celebration.

EDITOR'S NOTE: *Here ends the first part of the story. What follows was probably added at a later time.*

There were other officers, however, who had not gone on the journey but instead had remained in Constantinople. When they learned of the heroes' return, the devil stirred up envy in their hearts. They implored their superior, the prefect, to help them falsely accuse the three ship officers of treason against Emperor Constantine. The prefect argued a convincing case, whereupon Constantine flew into a rage and sent the three officers to prison without trial. They were to be beheaded that very night!

"Alas," warned the friendly jail warden. "You are sentenced to die. Make your final peace!" The officers tore their clothes and their hair in grief. But then one of them remembered how St. Nicholas had helped the other three falsely accused sailors in Myra. Desperately, he begged his two companions to pray to St. Nicholas, this time on their own behalf.

The good Saint heard their prayers. That very night Nicholas appeared to the emperor in a dream, commanding him in a stern voice to free the three officers. Constantine would be torn apart by wild beasts, Nicholas threatened, if he did not obey. The Saint then appeared to the prefect and likewise ordered *him* to free the innocent men, or else fall ill and become food for worms, along with his entire family!

The next morning, Constantine and the prefect told one another of their nightly visions. They decided to hold a public hearing with the three prisoners, at which Constantine was quite ready to accuse them again: "You must have some mysterious dark magic by which you conjure apparitions to come in the night and frighten people," he exclaimed angrily. But the officers replied, "Indeed not, we know no magic!" The emperor mentioned that the apparition had said its name was *Nicholas*. Did they know of any *Nicholas*? Of course they did—and how happy they were to learn that he had answered their prayers! The officers quickly explained how Nicholas had also saved the three innocent sailors at Myra.

Convinced at last, Constantine freed the three officers, observing that it was not he but rather this Nicholas who should be credited for saving their lives. The emperor himself ordered the men to give thanks to their saintly benefactor—as if they needed any encouragement! Then he rewarded them with golden treasures and sent them on their way.

Joyfully, the officers returned to Myra to venerate St. Nicholas. There they distributed their new wealth among the poor and devoted themselves to charitable work for many, many years.

The Legend of Stilling the Tempest

EDITOR'S NOTE: *Readers will recognize this legend as the one appearing on the cover of this book depicting* St. Nicholas *as the patron saint of sailors. It has been one of the most widely painted of all the legends about* St. Nicholas *and is next in importance to* "The Legend *of the* Three Stratilates." *Its events are said to have occurred while the* Bishop *of* Myra *was still alive. In the* West, *it appeared first in the writings of* John *the* Deacon.

Once, many long years ago, some sailors were caught in a heavy storm at sea and thought they were surely about to perish in the mountainous waves. They had heard of the miracles in Nicholas's name. In desperation, they cried out to him for help.

Much to their amazement, right away the vision of a man appeared to them in the air above their heads! With superhuman ability, he immediately took over the navigation of the ship. Soon the sails filled, the deck steadied, and, to the sailors' great relief, the storm abated. Then the unknown man disappeared just as suddenly as he had come into sight.

After they had landed successfully in Myra, the sailors went to the church to give thanks for the miracle of their rescue. But they were soon amazed again when they recognized the Bishop standing before them as the very man who

had answered their prayers in such a wonderful way. They would have fallen at the Bishop's feet, but he took their hands and bade them stand.

"It was not through me that your lives were saved," he said modestly, "but through the power of your faith and the grace of God."

ROMANIAN FOLKTALE

St. Nicholas Finds the Path

EDITOR'S NOTE: *Here we encounter* St. Nicholas *as the protector of maidens. Once again, we find it unusual that a traditional folktale should have been passed down to us in the voice of a first-person narrator—in this case, that of a woman remembering a remarkable adventure she had as a teenager in the mountains of* Romania.

Many years ago, when we were very young, I belonged to a group of six or seven girls so close that we were like sisters. Every late summer, after we had brought in the harvest, we usually made a special journey, a pilgrimage to one of the cloisters—Moldivitza, Humor, Putna—not too far from home. On one such trip, something happened that all of us have never forgotten, even though it took place a long time ago.

We were on our way home, hiking from Putna over the mountains, when we met a man who took pains to give us a warning. He said we were headed for a forest path that no one should take in that season, because the leaves were so thick that the woods were very dark. He said it would be difficult, if not impossible, to find the way out.

But we girls felt safe in our large group. We had sometimes gotten lost on other hikes, but we had always found our way again. Besides, what could we do

now? We had already gone a good part of the way. The path the man didn't want us to take was the shortest route. To avoid it, we would have had to turn back, and none of us wanted to do that.

So we kept walking. When we came to the path that led into the forest, we took it without a moment's hesitation—through the dense trees and up the mountainside.

We soon discovered the man had been right about one thing: The forest *was* really dark—and spooky. There were no villages, nor even isolated houses or cabins, and we saw no people. Every now and then, we heard the sound of axes cutting wood. Knowing that woodcutters must be nearby put us somewhat at ease, and we walked on resolutely, trying not to worry.

At twilight, we came upon a ramshackle hermitage next to a spring-fed well. Grateful for this sign of life, we ate our supper in the little clearing and washed. Then, just as the light was fading, we entered the broken-down chapel. The hermitage was locked, but the church door was open.

Inside, we called out to announce ourselves, but there was no answer. The place seemed deserted, which was all the more eerie in that we found four small oil lamps burning in front of some very old paintings. One stood in front of Our Lord Jesus Christ, one in front of the Mother of God, one in front of St. Nicholas—and the fourth, I've now forgotten.

We kneeled and prayed and sang hymns as we usually did. Then, suddenly weary, we lit candles to find a place to sleep. The floor of the church was stony and covered with branches; it looked like a most uncomfortable bed.

Searching around, by our flickering candlelight we found stairs leading upward. We had to climb them carefully in our flickering candlelight, because the steps were in such bad shape. But at least the floor above was made of wood. Even though it was dusty, it promised to be a better place to sleep than the cold stone floor below.

We prepared to lie down, but one of us discovered that the wooden wall had a door that sprang open when we pressed it. After that, who was tired? Never mind that the door made a great creaking sound. One after the other, we entered into a short, dark passage and cautiously felt our way to another door at the end. This one opened with a latch.

What followed was very strange and mysterious. We walked on through many doors into a series of rooms filled with all kinds of objects. Even in the dim light of our candles, we could see they were precious: gold and silver angels, filigree ornaments, brocade curtains, brightly colored cloths and rolled rugs, porcelain dishes, and pewter goblets.

At first, we stared at everything in awed silence. Then one of us whispered, "Shouldn't we take a picture or some small thing as a souvenir?"

"What are you thinking?" another answered. "You mustn't steal anything from this sacred place!"

"Yes, but we could give it to the nuns in the cloister."

"No, you can't do that!"

"Shhhh!"

At last, exhausted from our long day's hike, we unrolled a large, soft rug in one of the rooms and quickly fell to sleep on it.

That night, curiously, some of the others and I dreamed the same dream—that we couldn't find the way out of those rooms. And when we were trying, we heard heavy footsteps behind us. Yet when we turned, no one was there!

And truly, when we awoke and lit the candles to leave, we all felt somewhat confused, rather as in a nightmare. Looking for the way out, we retraced our steps. But instead of finding the upper passage we had come through, we discovered to our great dismay that now the hall led to a door opening onto a steep stone stairwell descending into darkness. We lit more candles, but couldn't see anything in their feeble glow, and we were afraid to climb down these steps.

Baffled, we decided to return to the room where we had slept. At least it would feel somewhat familiar, and then we could think about what to do. But when we turned around, we couldn't even find the place we had so recently left! The corridor looked the same, except that now where we were certain the door to our room had been, there was only a solid wall. Our hearts began to pound. We held hands for courage. Even the bravest among us felt like crying, especially when we heard footsteps, just as we had in our dream.

Then suddenly a door swung open from the other side of the hallway! We shrank back, terrified. But from the shadows emerged merely a white-haired and white-bearded monk! His lamp cast a warm, sunny glow on his friendly face. Smiling, he asked, "Girls, you look as if you need some help. Are you lost?"

"Yes," we answered breathlessly. "We slept here, needing shelter. We meant no harm, and now we want to go home."

The monk spoke kindly, "I heard you singing and praying yesterday. You did well not to take any of the things you saw. Come; I will show you the way."

He led us through a series of rooms that were all dark, even though it must have been broad daylight outside. At last we were standing on the landing at the top of the stairs. The monk blew out his lamp, and we blew out our candles.

We went down the steps and prayed before the icon of the Mother of God. The small oil lamps were still burning in front of her picture and of that of Our Lord. But the lamp in front of the painting of St. Nicholas had gone out, and the image was too hidden in shadows to see clearly.

When we had finished praying, we left the little church, followed by the monk. He accompanied us through the forest until we came to a side path, where he said, "This is the way you must take to get to where you are going."

But we had never *told* him where we were going! How did he know?

We set off in that direction, but had only gone a few steps before we turned around to thank our benefactor. But the monk wasn't there! We ran back to the other path and looked in both directions, but no one was there, anywhere.

Once more, we seemed to be dreaming. What a mystery! In the midst of our bewilderment, one of us exclaimed, "Girls, remember the figure in the painting last night? He had a white beard and white hair and was wearing a cloak, just like our monk!"

And fifty years later, to this very day, my friends and I still believe that the man who helped us was St. Nicholas himself.

DUTCH FOLKTALE

St. Nicholas Retrieves the Ball

Narrated by H. van Noenen

EDITOR'S NOTE: *The emphasis on* St. Nicholas *as the protector of children is a hallmark of his character. The situations change with the passage of time. For instance, this next story seems to be a more modern folktale, given the urban setting and the broken window. The power of the icon is still there. The story is considered a folktale, even though it is attributed to a narrator,* H. *van* Noenen, *about whom we know nothing, other than that he was probably* Dutch.

It was a perfect autumn day in a little Dutch town. The sun was warm on the face, in spite of the late season, and the remaining leaves were ablaze with color in the clear sky. Cheeks flushed with excitement, some boys were playing soccer on a quiet side street. One of them, in his enthusiasm, kicked the ball through a windowpane of a nearby house.

The man who lived in that house had always complained about those boys and their noise. They didn't dare ring his doorbell right away. Finally, the boy who had kicked the ball mustered his courage and rang the bell. When the door swung open, the owner of the house greeted him with a rug beater in his hand.

"Please, sir, may I have our ball back? I am very sorry for your trouble," the boy said politely.

"The only thing *you* may have is a beating!" replied the angry man. "You won't get your ball. Now, at last, I can have some peace!"

He slammed the door behind the boy, who had already turned and run to rejoin his friends. They stood there in dismay, unable to make a plan.

Finally, someone said, "Let's go ask St. Nicholas for help."

Soon they were standing in the empty, dimly lit church, in front of a large portrait of the Saint. One of the boys spoke: "Please, St. Nicholas, *please* help us to get our ball back. We promise not to be so careless again."

For a long moment, all was silent. Then, much to the boys' astonishment, the image said, "Don't worry! I'll come with you and we'll get that ball."

"But how, Father Nicholas?" the boys gasped. "You are a painting! You can't come down from out of the picture."

"Well, well, so I am! I suppose not. But who is standing behind you?"

The boys spun around to find an older man with a white beard, in a dark coat, hat in hand, looking just like the portrait of St. Nicholas.

"Now, come with me, boys!" said the old gentleman.

The boys looked at each other in wonder as the old man, without asking for directions, led them straight to the house with the broken window. "Stay here," he cautioned. Then he rang the doorbell.

"What do *you* want?" grumbled the man of the house.

"If you please, I would like to have the boys' ball," came the reply.

"Those bad boys can't have the ball. And they must pay for the broken window, besides," shouted the man.

"Ah, yes—the broken window. Where is it, please?" the old man asked.

"Come and see for yourself," said the owner. He led his visitor to the window where the ball had entered, but none of the panes were broken. Shaking his head, he went to another window, but not a single piece of glass there was broken, either.

"Strange!" he cried out in surprise.

"Perhaps the window was open and the boys' ball simply flew in," the old gentleman suggested.

"Definitely not. During the day, I keep the windows closed because of the noise and the dirt. When the ball came, I heard a crash and found the glass shattered on the floor!"

"Well, well," the old gentleman replied sympathetically. "We've all confused things. And we all made mistakes when we were young. But as you can see, nothing is damaged. Give me the ball, please, and I'll tell the boys to play someplace else. They'll do as I ask—you can count on it."

"Yes, of course." Now rather confused, the man nodded in agreement and handed over the ball.

The old man stroked his white beard and said, smiling, "You are very kind. On behalf of the boys, I thank you very much."

When the old man returned to the street, the boys crowded around him, wanting to know everything that had happened. He wouldn't say, but with a flourish, handed the errant ball to the very youth who had kicked it through the window. How did he know which boy it was? But moments later they all forgot the question, as the old man—remembering what it was to be full of energy on a warm autumn day—suddenly exclaimed, "You mustn't play here anymore, but I know a better place nearby. Come with me!"

"To see the heathen dragon."

"What do you want from him?"

"Marko the Rich Man has sent me to find out how much wealth he has."

"No, my friend!" warned the dragon's mother. "That is not why you are here. Marko knows very well that if my son has the chance, he will certainly eat you!"

The boy fell to his knees at her feet. "Dear grandmother, please do not let me die a bitter death. I was sent here against my will!"

"Now, now! I will not lead you into bad luck. I myself will ask the dragon your question."

"Then please also ask him this: The ferryman who brought me across the sea has worked there for thirty years and wants to know who will relieve him."

"Very well, I will ask that question also."

"And then, dear grandmother, I have one more question. I saw a pillar of gold that reached from heaven to earth. Whose gold is it?"

"We shall see! Now I must think quickly about where to hide you!" The old woman looked this way and that and finally tucked the boy under the feather bed.

SWOOOSH! Soon the dragon returned, hungry and ill-tempered because he had not found anyone to devour. The moment he entered the house, he began sniffing the air. "My dear mother, is anyone with you? I smell Russian flesh!"

"You have flown across the wide world and smelled *many* Russians! Now you imagine things. Come, would you like to drink a cup of tea, my little son?"

"Yes, my good mother," the dragon said.

The old woman secretly put some intoxicating drops into the dragon's tea. Then she gave him a second cup. And a third. Thoroughly drunk, the dragon asked, "My little mother, don't you have more?"

She gave him one more glass and his head began to feel light. Then his mother said, "Listen, my son, to my questions. How much money does Marko the Rich Man have?"

"Why would you know, my dear mother?"

"Just to satisfy my curiosity, my dear son."

"Even I can't count it. Marko can pile up his money for a distance of twenty five wersts in all four directions."

"Now tell me this: Across the sea is a ferryman. He has been there for thirty years. Who will relieve him?"

"Why do you wish to know, dear mother?"

"Just to have the answer, dear boy."

"Marko the Rich Man will relieve him."

"Excellent. Now tell me: On such and such a path, there is a pillar of gold coins that reaches from heaven to earth. To whom will this treasure belong?"

The dragon smiled dizzily and said, "Marko the Rich Man has an adopted son, my dear mother. The money will be given to him."

And with that, SWOOOSH! The heathen dragon flew away—God knows where he went!

The old woman rushed to uncover the feather bed and let the boy stand up. "Did you hear what the dragon said?"

"Yes, my grandmother."

"Now go home, my friend, and be well."

The boy thanked the old woman and started on his way. Soon he came to the pillar of gold coins that reached from heaven to earth. It asked, "Boy, did you find the answer to my question? To whom do I belong?"

"Yes! You belong to the adopted son of Marko the Rich Man."

AZZZZZZZZT! In an instant, the pillar fell to the ground in a huge pile. "Now I am yours," it said.

The boy played with the coins, but did not take the treasure with him. Instead, he left it there and walked on until he came to the sea.

"Do you know who will relieve me?" the ferryman asked?

"Yes! It is Marko the Rich Man."

"Is that so?" the ferryman marveled.

The ferryman took the boy across the sea, and the youth continued walking until he arrived home. Marko almost fainted to see his adopted son in such good health. "Did you find the heathen dragon," he asked.

"Yes, my father."

"How much money do I have?"

"In all four directions, your money would cover the earth for a distance of twenty-five wersts."

"Is that so!" the Rich Man marveled.

Soon Marko took the boy to another land where they sold their wares. Marko bought more goods and loaded them on a ship on the Volga River, arranging to send his adopted son home with them. Handing the boy a sealed letter he had written, he said, "Give this to my wife and daughter."

The boy dropped the letter in a cloth pouch and kept it close to his chest as the ship sailed up the Volga. At noon, the crew stopped to prepare lunch, and the boy got off the ship and walked along the bank. There he met an old man herding his sheep who called to him: "Come here, my good boy! Let me read the letter you're holding on your chest."

"It's my father's letter to his family. If you read it, who can seal it again?"

"I'll seal it."

The boy handed the letter in its pouch to the old man. After reading it, the shepherd tore it into little pieces. Then he wrote a new letter, which he dropped into the pouch and gave to the boy, saying, "Go with God!"

At the end of his journey, the boy delivered the rich man's wares; then he handed the letter to his mother. In Marko's handwriting, it said their daughter should marry their adopted son. The mother called the girl to read the letter, upon which she said, "Whatever dear father commands must be done!"

They held the wedding right away. No beer was needed, nor schnapps. Everything else was all in readiness for the ceremony. The bride and groom were led to the church, married among all the flowers abloom in that season, and then brought to their bedchamber.

Just at that time, Marko returned. "Wife, where is my adopted son?"

"We have just taken them to their marriage bed."

"What? Who!? "

"As you instructed, I have had him marry our daughter."

Marko could not hold back his fury. He spat in his wife's face and cried, "You stupid woman! What have you done?"

His wife handed him the letter, which he read in great bewilderment. It *was* in his handwriting, but it was not what he had written. In the first letter—the one the old shepherd tore to bits—Marko had ordered that his adopted son be taken to guard the suet factory at night and that all the boilers be filled with boiling fat. The boy had never been in the factory. If the fat boiled over, he would drown, Marko thought, because he would not be able to find the escape passage.

But the shrewd old shepherd had exchanged Marko's letter for a different one. The shepherd's beard was long and white, and his step was strong. Otherwise, he looked just like one of those beggars Marko had turned away many years ago. He was, in fact, St. Nicholas himself, just as the wise shepherdess had known.

Marko the Rich Man, of course, knew nothing of these matters. He could only fume inwardly when the young couple emerged from their bedroom, kissing in their happiness. His rage doubled when his adopted son said brightly, "My dear father, you own much money but God has given me even more!"

"Where is it?" Marko asked greedily.

The son told the story of the pillar of gold that had reached from heaven to earth and now lay in a pile, awaiting his return. Marko made haste to prepare three pairs of horses, and then the two men drove them to the sea where the ferryman took them across. After packing the treasure, they went back to the ferry. The rich man was pleased until they touched the far shore. But then, for him, the dragon's prediction came painfully true. As his new son-in-law led the horses away, Marko was forced to replace the ferryman, now free at last. For many years, Marko had to ferry the people back and forth across the sea, and back and forth again. Eventually, he died. His entire wealth—too great to count, stretching for twenty-five wersts in all directions—was given to his son-in-law. The young man took care of it and shared it well. He brought great joy and peace and relieved much suffering among the people. And he lived a long and happy life with the daughter of Marko the Rich Man.

V.P. Mohn.

LISA WENGER

St. Nicholas's Donkey

EDITOR'S NOTE: *This story has been taken from a novel by the German author,* Lisa Wenger. *Instead of a naughty boy, here we have a mischievous donkey, right to the sassy pun at the end of the story!*

Every child knows that St. Nicholas has a donkey. It is this gentle animal that carries the countless sacks full of nuts, apples, spice cookies, and other treats when his master rewards the children on St. Nicholas Day for being good throughout the year.

During the many years that St. Nicholas has visited the towns and villages, he hasn't always had the *same* donkey. But he has always had a donkey from the same *family*—after a father donkey retired, his son would take his place in stomping through the snow. These generations of donkeys have almost always looked like one another: All have been a beautiful silver-gray color, with a black mane and a little black braid in their tails. And all have been industrious and obedient, as is becoming for a donkey of St. Nicholas.

One year, when the snow was falling in thick flakes and Christmas was approaching, St. Nicholas went to the stall, patted his donkey's smooth back, and said, "Now, my gray one, shall we make our trip again?"

Children on Donkey, *German card circa* 1900

The donkey stamped his feet and brayed quietly. Then they set forth together—the donkey loaded down with sacks of presents and St. Nicholas keeping warm in his thick coat, high boots, and big fur gloves.

As they crossed the fields, the snow crunched under their feet and their breath flew around them in big clouds. But St. Nicholas laughed, looking out into the world with his happy old eyes, and the donkey shook with pleasure so that the silver bell around his neck could be heard far across the countryside.

The cold air made them both hungry, so they stopped at an inn in the very next village. After feeding his donkey in the stall, St. Nicholas went into the warm dining room for a bowl of soup.

Out in the stable, several horses waited for their masters, another donkey among them. In the stall just next to our friend was a big donkey that belonged to a miller.

"What kind of a fellow are *you*?" asked the miller's donkey in disdain.

"Me? I am St. Nicholas's donkey!" answered our gray one, with great pride.

"So!" said the miller's haughty donkey. "Aren't you special! Always running behind the old man, standing in front of the houses in the snow, almost freezing and starving before you come to your stall again. Not enough wages; always the same food—year in, year out. I just wouldn't take it!"

"Do you have it any better?" asked our donkey. "Surely you have to carry sacks, too! What about that?"

"Naturally," boasted the other donkey, "but only if I want to. And in the meantime, I run around and go wherever I want. If I am hungry, I come home and eat, but not your poor hay. No! I prefer oats, with bread and sugar!"

The little donkey believed everything this upstart said. After all, as St. Nicholas's helper, he had learned not to lie or to expect lies from others. He envied the life the big donkey described. He himself got oats and bread and sugar only on very rare occasions.

"It wasn't always this way," the miller's donkey continued. "One time, I simply ran away. I didn't come home for eight days. Since then, they let me do what I want. You know what? You should do the same! Why don't you run away from your old man and let him carry his sacks by himself? You'll see how much better he will treat you afterwards. Run, run! The door is open now, and you are not tied up!"

Nicholas's donkey, who really was very good, felt confused by these new ideas. But the big donkey's respect was important to him, and he had a genuine desire to make a trip on his own. It wasn't long before he had left his stall and walked straight out the stable door.

Once outside, he happily galloped across the road, through the potato fields, and into the forest. Oh, how thrilling it was to be free! He jumped this way and that, raced with the rabbits, played with the deer, and shook off the snow that fell from the evergreens onto his back.

"Caw, caw! It's St. Nicholas's donkey!" called a couple of ravens that the Saint had often seen when he was out in the country. "How did you get here?"

"All by myself," the donkey said proudly. "Soon I'll go home again. But for right now, I'm fed up with carrying sacks, and I want a little freedom."

"And St. Nicholas?" asked the deer and the elk and the rabbits. "Have you thought about him?"

"Oh, him!" the naughty donkey said. "Now he will have to look for another donkey or carry his sacks himself."

The donkey traveled further into the forest. There he met a young man with a gun who had killed two rabbits.

"You've come at just the right moment!" the man laughed. Before the donkey realized what was happening, the man had jumped onto his back. All the little beast's bucking was useless.

For what seemed like hours, the fellow goaded the donkey with the sharp heels of his boots through the woods to the next village, where he finally climbed off. Tired and hungry, the donkey ran away into a big meadow, looking for something to eat. The snow was very high and frozen; there was not even a tiny weed to be found.

At the edge of the forest, the donkey saw an old woman carrying a big load of wood on her back. She seemed in pain, breathing heavily and walking with great effort. Our donkey, who had learned only kindness from St. Nicholas, went over to the old woman and stood in front of her. Dropping his head, he looked at her in such an encouraging way that she understood him. In a moment, the old woman had loaded her wood onto his back. "Ah!" she said, scratching his neck gratefully. Then our little donkey trotted behind her until they reached her cottage at some distance from the village.

The wood was hardly unloaded when the old woman's grandchildren jumped around the donkey and called out, "Oh, let me ride, let me ride!"

The donkey had learned from St. Nicholas to love children, and so he did let them ride. He carried first the girls, then the boys, then the girls, and then the boys again, who called out "Getty-up!" and "Whoa!" merrily waving their caps. Finally, at the edge of the village the donkey threw them off in the soft snow banks; and as the children ran home the sounds of laughter filled the air.

The donkey continued on his way alone, but he didn't know where he should go. He was tired and hungry and thirsty. He came to a fountain, but the water was frozen except for a few drops dripping from the wooden pipe. Licking it did not quench his thirst. Nor could he find anything to eat.

Slowly he walked back into the forest, thinking about his warm stall and the delicious hay that St. Nicholas had always fed him. All of a sudden he missed his good master, who patted his back so often. On he plodded through the woods, feeling sadder and sadder. Here, there, a pinecone dropped, or a dry branch cracked, but otherwise it was quite still—too still! Twilight came, making the twisted limbs of the bare trees look spooky. If only he knew the way! If only he was home again, he thought sorrowfully. And his head sank. . . .

Meanwhile, after St. Nicholas had eaten his soup, he went out to the stall to get his donkey. But, of course, the donkey wasn't there. St. Nicholas looked everywhere and asked everybody about his four-legged friend, but no one had seen him. Out into the street he went looking, and over to the potato field. There, at last he noticed some tracks of small hoofs in the snow and began to follow them. High overhead, a couple of ravens croaked, "Your donkey is in the forest!" Then they flew in front of St. Nicholas and showed him the way.

But since the crows had seen him, the donkey had been on his grand adventure. Soon they no longer knew where to look, but just then the elk appeared and said, "St. Nicholas, your donkey has returned to the village."

Already out of breath, St. Nicholas ran back the way he had come. Suddenly, a hare hopped across his path, sitting on his haunches straight up like a candle. "St. Nicholas," he said, "your donkey is behind the village in the forest. I just saw him. He is standing under a pine tree with drooping ears."

And so it was. When St. Nicholas climbed the hill behind the village, he found his dejected donkey standing there. The little beast was so tired and forlorn that he didn't even turn his head when he heard his master's steps.

"My gray friend!" called St. Nicholas.

Then how quickly the donkey's head came up! Even in the dark, he recognized St. Nicholas immediately. How he jumped and ran to him! He rubbed his head on his beloved master's familiar fur coat and brayed and brayed.

"But, my gray one," St. Nicholas said softly, "Where have you been? What have you been doing?"

The donkey hung his head, terribly ashamed.

St. Nicholas put on his halter, and the two good friends trudged happily through the snow to the next inn. There, the Saint led the donkey to the innkeeper's stable and placed a full bale of hay in his stall. And when at last the donkey stood safe and warm on clean straw, with the fragrant hay in front of him and St. Nicholas scratching him behind the ears, he thought to himself, "This time, Gray One, you weren't a donkey. You were really an ass!"

Detail from Saint Nicholas with Scenes from His Life, *Russian, 16th century*

PART THREE

Bread and Cookies

The Legend of the Three Grain Ships

EDITOR'S NOTE: *This legend, as is also true of many of the folktales, depicts a situation in which the people are hungry. Nicholas, as the patron saint of grain traders, is first and foremost a nurturer and provider for those in dire need.*

Once it happened that the people of St. Nicholas's whole province of Lycia were starving, for their grain storehouses were almost empty. Then the Saint heard that three ships loaded with grain had arrived, and so he hurried to the harbor. "Please!" he begged the captains. "My people are hungry. You would serve them and God greatly by giving a hundred bushels of grain from each of your ships."

The three captains answered, "Father, we dare not, for the grain is distributed to us by measure, and we must deliver that same measure to the emperor's storehouses in Alexandria upon peril of death."

"Do as I ask you," the holy man said to them, "and I promise your grain shall not be diminished when you come to the storehouses."

Detail from Meeting of St. Nicholas with the Imperial Messenger and the Salvage of the Ship with Grain *by Fra Angelico, 15th century*

The three captains did as St. Nicholas had requested, measuring out to him a hundred bushels of grain from each of their ships. Then the Saint portioned out the grain to each man, woman, and child according to need, so that it was enough for two years, not only to live on but also to plant. From then on, the people suffered from hunger no more.

And when the three ships sailed into Alexandria, they did indeed deliver to the emperor the full measure with which they had first set forth.

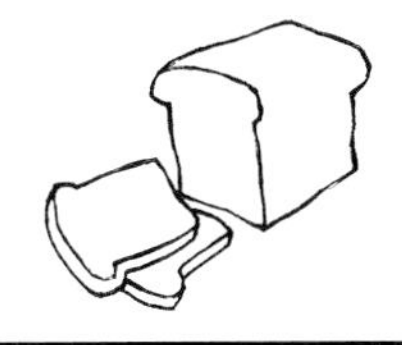

GREEK FOLKTALE

The Icon's Warm Bread

EDITOR'S NOTE: *What is tragic is that in poor places, children are still sent out to beg, exactly as depicted in this old Greek folktale. Let us hope that* St. Nicholas *will be their protector as he is for the children here.*

Once there was a brother and sister whose parents had suddenly died, leaving the poor children all alone in the world—or almost all alone. They did have an uncle who lived not far away, and even though the children scarcely knew him, the townsfolk took them to him, since he was their only living relative.

"Don't cry," the people comforted the sad boy and girl. "Your uncle is your family now, and he will take care of you. You must be brave and good for him."

This uncle was a wealthy man, owning many cattle and a large house filled with fine possessions. Little did the townsfolk know he was a mean and stingy man. Far from caring for the children, he was angry with them for still being so small—too young to be useful servants and not yet strong enough to manage heavy work.

But there was one thing they were not too small for—begging! Every morning, the uncle sent the children out onto the streets to beg for money, and

St. *Nicholas cookie mold, German, late* 16*th century*

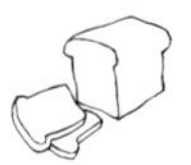

every evening he made them hand over every drachma they had collected as soon as they came home.

And that is how life was. With bare feet and cheeks flushed with hunger, the little beggars would stand all day on the street corners, holding out their cups to those who passed by. Some compassionate and kind people gave the children money or bread, but others were hard hearted and gave nothing. Some even made fun of the waifs or shook their heads in disapproval.

One rainy day the children had received almost nothing. As evening approached, the rain stopped and the sun came out from behind the clouds, but the small beggars looked at their empty cups in dismay, fearing their uncle's bad temper. Strangely enough, just then a well-dressed man appeared and gave each of them a large silver coin. The children had never seen such large coins. How they gleamed in the fading light! As the gentleman strode away, the brother and sister shouted their thanks to him and then said happily, "Today, for once, Uncle will surely praise us!"

As soon as evening came, they started off, eager to go home. But from a distance, two older boys had seen the gentleman take money from his pocket and give it to the children. These boys waited in the shadows until the children passed. Then they grabbed the defenseless little ones and took everything they had—including the gentleman's large silver coins.

The brother and sister ran home crying and told their uncle what had happened. "Get out!" the man screamed, chasing them from the house. "Disappear, you worthless little thieves! I never want to see you again!"

The terrified children ran out into the dark, dashing first one way, and then another. They did not know where to go or what to do. Finally, they happened to come to the street where the church was. Seeing its windows were lit, they went in.

Inside, the sanctuary glowed in the flickering light of many candles. The exhausted children began to cry with relief at being in what they felt was a safe place. The first thing they noticed was an icon of St. Nicholas. Through their tears, and in the shimmering light of the candles, it seemed to them that in the

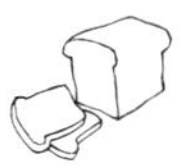

painting the Saint's lips began to move. An instant later they were surprised to hear a deep, kind voice say, "Children, are you hungry?"

"Yes, very hungry!" the astonished children managed to reply.

"Here, then, take this." In the unsteady light, the children couldn't be sure, but they thought they saw the robed arms of the icon move. Regardless, the delicious aroma filling the room was real enough, and so were the three warm pieces of bread the children suddenly found in their hands.

The image of St. Nicholas continued, "I know you were chased out of your home. So be it! You have nothing more to fear from that miser of an uncle. Go now to the little house down the road." He pointed to show them the direction. "Give the old woman who lives there one of these pieces of bread and tell her that I sent you. She will take you in."

The children thanked St. Nicholas and did as he had instructed. Sure enough, when they gave the old woman the bread and said Nicholas had sent them, she welcomed them in. Her house was not grand like their uncle's, and her possessions were modest and few. But her heart was much larger, and the children knew they had found a home at last.

The next day, they went back to the church to thank St. Nicholas again. Once more, he gave them three pieces of bread and said: "Come as often as you are hungry!"

In this way the children and the old woman lived for some time. Every day, the boy and girl shared the Saint's bread with the old woman, and she in her turn cared for them well.

Then, quite unexpectedly, the stingy uncle died in an accident. As it so happened, the children inherited his house, his cattle, and all his possessions. When they returned to what was now their new home, they took the old woman with them. They continued to give thanks to St. Nicholas whenever they passed the church. Now, though, he didn't need to offer them any more bread, because they had plenty to eat at home.

As time passed, the old woman became too frail to take care of the children any longer. But by then they were grown and took loving care of her.

A Merry Christmas

RECIPE FOR

Grittibenz

(ST. NICHOLAS BREAD)

EDITOR'S NOTE: *While I was a teacher in Zürich, Switzerland, St. Nicholas Day was always a time of informal celebrations with refreshments. On December 6, teachers and students alike spent the first school period eating tangerines, nuts, and the special foot-long* Grittibenz St. Nicholas *bread. Traditionally served on St. Nicholas Day in Switzerland, this bread is easy and fun to make. Children love to watch the dough rise.*

Ingredients:

4 packages activated dry yeast
1 teaspoon vanilla
1 teaspoon salt
1/2 teaspoon grated orange rind
1/2 cup granulated sugar
4–5 cups all-purpose flour
3 eggs
1/2 cup softened butter or margarine
raisins and nuts for decoration

Norwegian Winterman *by* English School, 19*th century*

Procedure:

(Preheat oven to 325°.)

1. Dissolve yeast in 1 cup lukewarm water; add salt and sugar.
2. Stir in eggs, vanilla, and orange rind.
3. Add enough flour to make soft dough.
4. Work in butter and add more flour if needed.
5. Let dough rest for 5 minutes.
6. Knead dough on floured surface until no longer sticky, about 5 minutes. Form into ball and place in a lightly floured bowl. Cover with towel and place in draft-free area to rise until dough doubles in bulk (about 30 minutes). The inside of an unlit oven is ideal. Dough has risen enough when it does not spring back to the touch.
7. Punch dough down and remove from bowl. Knead briefly, 3 or 4 times, on lightly floured surface and divide into fourths, forming each fourth into oblong shape.
8. Cut 1/4 of dough off bottom of each oblong shape (to use for heads and decorations).
9. Cut bottom half of each oblong vertically and shape to form legs and feet.
10. Shape heads, suspenders, and belt from cut-off dough and attach to body. Raisins and nuts may be used to make eyes, mouths, buttons, etc.
11. Brush each figure with egg yolk diluted with a little water.
12. Bake in 325° oven for 25–30 minutes.

GERMAN FOLKTALE

The Pfeffernüsse

EDITOR'S NOTE: Pfeffernüse *literally means "spice cookie" in German. In all good humor, we feel we need to alert you that this story, like the cookie, is a bit spicy, but just as great a favorite. Before reading it, all listeners, young and old, would do well to practice the donkey call:* EEE-AH!

Once upon a time, St. Nicholas was traveling through the provinces of the lower Rhine. When he arrived at the outskirts of the city of Düren, he saw a small chapel and suddenly felt a call to worship there.

"Stay here, my friend," he said to his donkey as he dismounted. Then he left it to graze freely on the rich green grass surrounding the chapel while he went inside. It wasn't long before he was deeply immersed in his devotions. . . .

Refreshed after praying so intently, St. Nicholas left the chapel to continue his journey. But now he could not find his donkey! He looked everywhere around the chapel, but the donkey wasn't there.

Not far away, on the banks of the river, some local fishermen were busy at work with their latest catch. Nicholas walked over and begged for their help. The good fishermen agreed, devising a plan to lure the donkey back.

The day was dark and overcast, so the men lit torches and held them high as they searched the fields and the roads and the streets. They also blew cow

Father Christmas *by Edith Scannell, early 20th century*

3. Beat eggs with granulated sugar until very thick and blend into the flour mixture.
4. Form into walnut-size balls. Place on lightly greased cookie sheet one inch apart.
5. Bake in 350° oven for 15–20 minutes or until cookies are firm and light brown in color.
6. Cool completely. Roll in powdered sugar.

Makes 180 one-inch balls.

IRISH FOLKTALE

A Small Fish Story

EDITOR'S NOTE: *We've hunted high and low and haunted libraries—including the greatest folklore library in North America at Indiana University in Bloomington—to find more stories about St. Nicholas from the British Isles. (The British figure is known instead as "Father Christmas.") This is the only story we've been able to locate. If anyone knows of others, please send them to us!*

While St. Nicholas was generous to others, he did not lead a grand life himself. He was even once a beggar who traveled all over the country with only the clothes on his back, his staff, and an old wooden pail. One day, he came to a little town by the sea where almost no one was willing to help him. All day he stood on the street, asking for alms. But by the time evening fell, only three people had taken pity on him: a fisherman, a woman, and a priest. Strangely enough, each of them had given him the same thing—not a coin, but a small fish.

He put all three fish in his pail filled with water and walked on until he came to a house where a very poor widow lived with her children.

"Begging your pardon, madam, but might a person stay here overnight?"

"To be sure," the widow answered wearily, "but we only have water soup and a crust of bread for supper."

"Supper won't be a problem! Look here: I have three fish. You can fry them and we and the children will all eat them together."

The widow looked doubtfully into the beggar's pail. She had no way of knowing the three little fish had been growing in there. By the time she saw them, they had become quite large.

"What a joy," the woman cried. "I haven't seen such big fish for a long time, not even at the market!"

One fish, two fish, three fish do I see,
Plenty for my children and enough for me!

She happily lit a fire and began to cook the fish over the glowing coals.

While she was about her work, the Saint asked, "Do you have a pail?"

"Yes, indeed I do."

"I'll thank you to fill it with water and bring it to me." The woman did as he asked. Soon the fish were ready to eat. And how delicious they were! The widow and her children were so hungry they left nothing but the bones.

Nicholas said, "Don't throw those bones away. Give them to me."

The children and their mother looked at one another in surprise. "What is he up to?" they whispered. But they were so grateful for a good meal at last that they didn't question Nicholas.

After they had eaten, the family lay the bones of all three fish on a plate. Nicholas picked up the bones by the tail and threw them into the widow's pail.

Again everyone was surprised. "Why is he doing that?" they wondered.

Then as the widow was about to carry the pail outside to empty it, she noticed three live fish swimming in the water! "What?" she gasped. "How could that be?"

One fish, two fish, three fish do I see,
Plenty for my children and enough for me!

Who knew where the fish came from but Nicholas, and by that time he was sound asleep.

The next morning, the good Saint said, "Please fix these fish for breakfast."

The woman gladly did so, and once again everyone had enough to eat.

When they were finished, again Nicholas said, "Bring me the pail and give me the bones." Then he threw them into the water and continued, "You must always do this. That way, you will always have fish and you and your children won't be hungry any more."

Then the Saint swung his wooden pail over the end of his staff, said good-bye, and walked off down the road.

The widow and her children never saw St. Nicholas again, but they lived well for a long time. At last, one day the mother left a single child alone at home while she and the others went to visit relatives. The child at home got hungry, so he tiptoed over to the widow's pail and looked in:

One fish, two fish, three fish do I see,
Enough for the others and PLENTY *for me*!

With that, he scooped out one of the fish and fried it for himself. Afraid that his mother would find out and scold him, he threw the bones away.

When the widow returned, the first thing she did was go to the pail to prepare dinner.

One fish, two fish, thr—

But now there were not three fish swimming in the water—there were only two. And from then on, that had to be plenty enough for all of them!

ITALIAN FOLKTALE

The Miller's Tail

EDITOR'S NOTE: St. Nicholas *has long been known as the patron saint of millers. Interestingly, the other stories in this collection that feature a miller—*"The Nicholas Ship" *and* "St. Nicholas's Donkey"*—also portray him as being rich. Because the miller's was the only mechanized profession in an agricultural society, he was usually wealthier than the neighboring farmers, and so disliked. Perhaps that explains why, at least since the time of the medieval* English *poet* Chaucer, *millers have been the object of humor in stories of various cultures. This* Italian *folktale is no exception.*

Many years ago there was a poor woman whose husband had died. She and her two children were all alone in the world and did not know where their next meal would come from. Indeed, the whole country was starving, and the woman was desperate because her neighbors had so little for themselves they could not help her.

Weak though they were, the widow led her children by the hand to church. Over their cries, while she was praying she heard a voice from the next altar: "Go to the windmill. There you will find bread and shelter."

Strange! The woman had thought the church was empty. She looked in the direction of the sound, but saw no one. All she could see was that the altar next to where she was kneeling was dedicated to St. Nicholas.

Saint Nicholas on His Donkey, *19th century* Dutch *illustration with details*

Feeling foolish for talking to the air, the woman said quietly, "Yes, but the miller is the stingiest man for miles around. He won't give us anything."

"We shall see," the voice seemed to say. "Just go."

The woman was too desperate to argue. Immediately she rose and led her children to the windmill. A cold rain had begun to fall, causing the children in their misery to cry even louder. By the time they arrived at the mill, all three of them were soaked through and through. The woman knocked loudly, but they had to wait outside, shivering in the chill air a long time until the door opened.

"What do you want?" the miller bellowed.

"As a gift of God if you please, sir, a piece of bread and shelter until the rain lets up."

"This is not a restaurant, you foolish woman! And we don't provide 'gifts of God.' Pay or get out!"

"But you can see that the children are freezing. I would pay if I could, but I have no money. Please, have mercy on us."

"Go away, or I'll let the dogs loose!"

Just at that moment, an old man appeared from nowhere and stepped through the open door out of the rain. He did not say a word, but touched the miller with his staff. In an instant, the stingy miller fell forward on all fours and began to change.

First the miller's face grew long, his teeth bucked out, and his ears became tall and pointed. Next his clothes dropped off, revealing the sturdy back of an animal and a straggly tail ending in a tuft of wiry gray hair. The widow couldn't believe it, but the miller had become a donkey!

"EEEWAGH," he cried in outrage.

"Now, good woman," said the old man, whom she suddenly recognized as St. Nicholas, "take the children inside. You'll find a warm meal on the table and comfortable beds for all of you. From now on, you will be in charge here."

"But, my lord," the woman said, "I know nothing about the mill!"

"Never mind," said St. Nicholas. "Tomorrow I'll send you a helper who will do everything. All you need to do is take care of the customers. Just charge a price that is fair. Everything else will be done. And you can rent out the donkey. I'll return in a year to make sure you are well."

With that, St. Nicholas harnessed the miller-turned-donkey and led him, still braying in loud dismay, to the barn. Then the Saint disappeared.

The woman did not know what to think. But who could think at all with such tempting aromas tickling her nose? She and her children ran to the kitchen. Much to their amazement, they found a wonderful meal already cooked and on the table—thick pasta with rich red sauce, big rounds of creamy cheese, freshly baked bread, and new greens, even though the season was late! The starving family said a hasty prayer and sat down to the feast. They hadn't eaten so well for a very long time. Then, tired after their full meal, they found three soft beds waiting for them, and they slept more soundly than they ever had in their lives.

The next morning, a young man appeared at the door. "This must be the helper St. Nicholas promised," the woman thought to herself.

"Good morrow!" the young man greeted her. "I'm supposed to run the mill for my food and wages."

As soon as he spoke, the woman sensed the young man was trustworthy. She knew that St. Nicholas was behind it all, and she was happy to have help in running the mill. But what about the miller? That he was now a donkey in his stall—*that* was the part she did not understand!

And so her new life began. Together, the woman and the young man ran the mill. Every day, the young man would harness the donkey and keep him hard at work. Many people brought their grain to be ground. Because the woman charged only modest prices, she had more and more customers. And every evening, the little household would gather around the table for a fine meal.

A year later, there was a knock on the door. Opening it, the widow recognized the old man who had helped her.

"Now we'll see how things are," St. Nicholas said. "Come to the barn."

They went to the stall where the donkey was tied up. "EEEWAGH," the beast cried. Then Nicholas touched him lightly with his staff. In an instant, the donkey was transformed back into the miller—except that now he had slightly

longer ears, slightly protruding teeth, and a little tuft of wiry gray hair on his balding head.

St. Nicholas eyed him sternly. "Well, now! What should we do? Can you be respectful and hire this woman as your assistant? Or would you rather be a donkey?"

"Yes—I mean, no!" the miller said with a sincere heart. "I realize that I was wrong. I will be glad to have the woman's help, and I won't turn poor people away from my door ever again."

"Excellent! But remember, I don't live far from here. If necessary, I can easily return."

But it wasn't ever necessary for St. Nicholas to come back. The miller had indeed learned his lesson. From then on, he made sure that the woman and her children were well treated. Later, he even gave the mill to the little family. As he grew older, he became known far and wide as one of the kindest men around—and one of the most pleasant looking, too, in spite of his odd little tuft of wiry gray hair!

A COLONIAL
DUTCH-AMERICAN LEGEND

The Baker's Dozen

Dramatized by Aaron Shepard

EDITOR'S NOTE: *We have already mentioned that* St. Nicholas *is the patron saint of bakers and that it was the Dutch who first brought the customs of* St. Nicholas *Day to America. This story of "The Baker's Dozen," here adapted by Aaron Shepard, may be the only legend featuring* St. Nicholas *to originate on American soil. We hope it will inspire you to have a reader's theater with family, classmates, or friends, followed by refreshments in the form of some fine* St. Nicholas *cookies, the recipe for which follows the play.*

ROLES: Narrator 1, Narrator 2, Narrator 3, Narrator 4, Baker, Woman, (Customers, Children, St. Nicholas)

NOTE: For best effect, please place Narrators 1 and 2 at far left (as seen from the audience), and 3 and 4 at far right.

NARR. 1: In the Dutch colonial town later known as Albany, New York, there lived a baker, Van Amsterdam, who was as honest as he could be.

NARR. 4: Each morning, he checked and balanced his scales, and he took great care to give his customers *exactly* what they paid for—not more, and not less.

Saint Nicholas, *circa* 1890 *by* Dutch School

NARR. 2: Van Amsterdam's shop was always busy, because people trusted him, and because he was a good baker as well. And never was the shop busier than in the days before December 6, when the Dutch celebrate St. Nicholas Day.

NARR. 3: At that time of year, people flocked to the baker's shop to buy his fine St. Nicholas cookies.

NARR. 1: Made of gingerbread, iced in red and white, they looked just like St. Nicholas as the Dutch know him—

NARR. 4: tall and thin, with a high, red bishop's cap, and a long, red bishop's cloak.

NARR. 2: One St. Nicholas Day morning, the baker was just ready for business, when the door of his shop flew open.

NARR. 3: In walked an old woman, wrapped in a long black shawl.

WOMAN: I have come for a dozen of your St. Nicholas cookies.

NARR. 1: Taking a tray, Van Amsterdam counted out twelve cookies. He started to wrap them, but the woman reached out and stopped him.

WOMAN: I asked for a dozen. You have given me only twelve.

BAKER: Madam, everyone knows that a dozen *is* twelve.

WOMAN: But I say a dozen is *thirteen*. Give me one more.

NARR. 4: Van Amsterdam was not a man to bear foolishness.

BAKER: Madam, my customers get *exactly* what they pay for—not more, and not less.

WOMAN: Then you may keep the cookies.

NARR. 2: She turned to go, but stopped at the door.

WOMAN: Van Amsterdam! However honest you may be, your heart is small and your fist is tight. *Fall again, mount again, learn how to count again!*

NARR. 3: Then she was gone.

NARR. 1: From that day, everything went wrong in Van Amsterdam's bakery.

NARR. 4: His bread rose too high or not at all.

NARR. 2: His pies were too sour or too sweet.

NARR. 3: His cakes crumbled or were chewy.

NARR. 1: His cookies were burnt or doughy.

NARR. 4: His customers soon noticed the difference. Before long, most of them were going to other bakers.

BAKER: (*to himself*) That old woman has bewitched me. Is this how my honesty is rewarded?

NARR. 2: A year passed.

NARR. 3: The baker grew poorer and poorer.

NARR. 1: Since he sold little, he baked little, and his shelves were nearly bare. His last few customers slipped away.

NARR. 4: Finally, on the eve before St. Nicholas Day, not one customer came to Van Amsterdam's shop.

NARR. 2: At day's end, the baker sat alone, staring at his unsold St. Nicholas cookies.

BAKER: I wish St. Nicholas could help me now.

NARR. 3: Then he closed his shop and went sadly to bed.

NARR. 1: That night, the baker had a dream. He was a boy again, one in a crowd of happy children. And there in the midst of them was St. Nicholas himself.

NARR. 4: The bishop's white horse stood beside him, its baskets filled with gifts. Nicholas pulled out one gift after another, and handed them to the children.

NARR. 2: But Van Amsterdam noticed something strange. No matter how many presents Nicholas passed out, there were always more to give.

NARR. 3: In fact, the more he took from the baskets, the more they seemed to hold.

NARR. 1: Then Nicholas handed a gift to Van Amsterdam. It was one of the baker's own St. Nicholas cookies!

NARR. 4: Van Amsterdam looked up to thank him, but it was no longer St. Nicholas standing there.

NARR. 2: Smiling down at him was the old woman with the long black shawl.

NARR. 3: Van Amsterdam awoke with a start. Moonlight shone through the half-closed shutters as he lay there, thinking.

BAKER: I always give my customers *exactly* what they pay for—not more, and not less. But why *not* give more?

NARR. 1: The next morning, St. Nicholas Day, the baker rose early.

NARR. 4: He mixed his gingerbread dough and rolled it out.

NARR. 2: He cut the shapes and baked them.

NARR. 3: He iced them in red and white to look just like St. Nicholas.

NARR. 1: And the cookies were as fine as any he had made.

NARR. 4: Van Amsterdam had just finished, when the door flew open. In walked the old woman with the long black shawl.

WOMAN: I have come for a dozen of your St. Nicholas cookies.

NARR. 2: In great excitement, Van Amsterdam counted out twelve cookies—

NARR. 3: and one more.

BAKER: In this shop, from now on, a dozen is thirteen.

WOMAN: (*smiling*) You have learned to count well. You will surely be rewarded.

NARR. 1: She paid for the cookies and started out. But as the door swung shut, the baker's eyes seemed to play a trick on him.

NARR. 4: He thought he glimpsed the tail end of a long red cloak.

NARR. 2: As the old woman foretold, Van Amsterdam *was* rewarded. When people heard he counted thirteen as a dozen, he had more customers than ever.

NARR. 3: In fact, Van Amsterdam grew so wealthy that the other bakers in town began doing the same.

NARR. 1: From there, the practice spread to other towns, and at last through all the American colonies.

NARR. 4: And this, they say, is how thirteen became the "baker's dozen"—

NARR. 2: a custom common for over a century,

NARR. 3: and alive in some places to this day.

EDITOR'S NOTE: *Traditionally, thirteen is often the symbolic number for transformation. See the discussion at the end of* "The Nine Questions" *in part* 4 *of this book.*

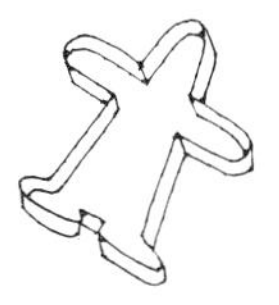

RECIPE FOR

Cut-Out Sugar Cookies

EDITOR'S NOTE: *This recipe is the best one we know for sugar cookies and makes enough for a family of four. The exact number depends on the thickness of the dough and the size of the cut-outs.*

Ingredients:

1 lb. softened butter, no substitutes
1 1/2 cups granulated sugar
5 cups all-purpose flour
3 egg yolks and 1 whole egg
powdered sugar
juice from fresh lemons

Procedure:
(Preheat oven to 325°.)

1. In a large bowl, cream butter and sugar, add egg yolks and egg. Mix until well blended.
2. Add flour gradually into creamed mixture until dough forms.
3. Divide dough in halves and chill for 1 hour.
4. On lightly floured surface, roll dough to 1/8-inch thickness. (If dough is sticky, knead in a little more flour until it is easy to handle.) Work with

one half of the dough at a time, keeping the rest refrigerated until ready to use.

5. Cut into desired St. Nicholas shapes using cookie cutters or stiff cardboard figures you have designed yourself. Scraps of dough may be used for a beard, eyes, buttons, etc. Get inspired!
6. Bake on lightly greased cookie sheet at 350 degrees for 5 to 7 minutes until light brown in color.
7. Cool slightly; remove from pan. Cool on rack.
8. For frosting, mix together powdered sugar and lemon juice, diluted by half with water, to reach spreadable consistency. Frost cookie and decorate as desired! (Of course, you may use your own frosting recipe, but the lemon in this one makes it particularly delicious.)

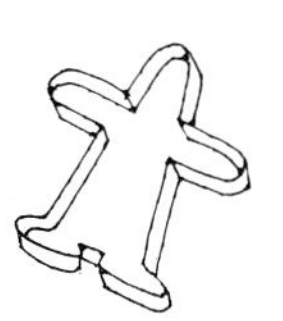

Detail from Saint Nicholas with Scenes from His Life, *Russian, 16th century*

PART FOUR

Tricks and Transformation

The Legend of the Seafaring Pilgrims

EDITOR'S NOTE: *The first legends of* St. Nicholas *come from the time of early Christianity when the old Greek gods and goddesses were rapidly losing favor. Symeon, as referenced in Jones, for instance, says that while* Nicholas *lived he tore down pagan temples and drove out the "demons" within them. Further, Jones tells us that churches dedicated to* Nicholas *were often built right on top of old temples devoted to the Greek goddess,* Artemis (Diana *in Roman mythology.*)[4] *In some sense* Nicholas *replaced* Artemis: *She was the goddess of the moon, and* Nicholas *frequently appears only at night and in dreams, just as we see in the legend here.* Nicholas *also replaced* Poseidon, *the Greek god of the sea, in his role as the protector of sailors.*

In the early days, pilgrims flocked from far and wide to visit Nicholas's tomb in Myra. Some lived in the furthest reaches of Asia Minor and had to travel long distances by sea to reach it.

At that time the land was still haunted by many demons whom Nicholas had driven out of the ancient temples where they once lived. One of these demons in particular kept an evil eye on all the pilgrims who wanted to journey to Nicholas's tomb instead of going to the old shrines. This jealous demon hated the new Saint who had toppled his goddess's temple and so made him

Detail from Destruction of the Oil of Diana *by Sebastian Daig, 16th century*

homeless. He paced back and forth until he came up with what he thought was a splendid plan to get even.

One day, a group of pilgrims were gathered at the port of their town, preparing for the long sea journey to Myra. As was the custom, they had brought jars filled with lamp oil so that when they arrived at Nicholas's tomb, they could light votive candles to honor him.

But the jealous demon was determined to prevent the blessings such devotion would bring them. Disguising himself as a fellow woman pilgrim, he appeared among them as they were loading their oil onto the ship. [We can imagine that "she" wore a large cap tied under her chin to hide pointed ears and a skirt that dragged on the ground to cover a curling tail.]

Feigning weakness, the demon-woman simpered, "I too would very much like to take my jar of lamp oil to the tomb of dear, good St. Nicholas, but alas, I am too ill to survive the long sea journey. Could you possibly present the jar for me? You are welcome to fill your own lamps with my fine oil, as a small payment for your trouble." [Perhaps at that very moment a small gust of wind came up and the speaker hastened to hold down her skirt and tuck in her tail.] The unsuspecting pilgrims took the jar and promised to do as the "sick woman" asked.

The first day of their voyage passed without incident. But during the night, Nicholas—who had been watching over the pilgrims all along—appeared to one of them and instructed him to throw the jar overboard, into the sea!

At dawn this pilgrim told the others, and they agreed at once. To their astonishment, no sooner had the jar struck the water than it burst into flames! The entire sky seemed to be on fire, and the most terrific stench filled the air. The waters began to split apart, writhing and foaming, and the stunned pilgrims heard deep rumblings, as in an earthquake. Waves much higher than the ship began to crash over the decks, and it soon began to sink as if it were a toy.

Surely this was no ordinary storm! Terrified, the pilgrims began to despair. How could they hope to be saved now, when it seemed they were all about to perish in the looming water!

But then suddenly St. Nicholas appeared before them. At that very moment, the fire began to die and the waves to subside. Swiftly but in complete safety, the ship miraculously glided away from the troubled spot. For the rest of the journey, Nicholas guided the ship smoothly under a gentle, fragrant breeze that took it straight along its course. It wasn't long before the city of Myra came into view, and the hearts of the pilgrims were filled with the greatest joy.

EDITOR'S NOTE: *Charles Jones calls this legend "Firebomb." According to him, word got around that* Nicholas *could control the devil's fire, and he became known as the protector against explosives. The legend also gives us an early example of what was known as* "Greek Fire," *an explosive substance that revolutionized warfare. Thought to have been invented by the engineer* Kallinikos *in* 678 A.D., *at first it was packed in clay jars and hurled onto enemy ship decks to break and explode on impact.*[5] *Later in the* Middle Ages, Nicholas *also became known as a protector and controller against* St. Elmo's Fire, *the meteorological phenomenon.*

ESTONIAN FOLKTALE

The Beautiful Crop of Rye

EDITOR'S NOTE: *The name* Ely *in this story is a version of* Elijah, *the Old Testament prophet. People often think of tricksters only in the negative sense of someone who deceives others for selfish ends or plays hurtful pranks, as sometimes happens on* Halloween. *But tricksters can also be positive figures who trick others to bring about helpful changes, as teachers and parents—and saints!—sometimes do.*

Long, long ago, there was a farmer so poor that he and his large family didn't have anything to eat. Disaster had befallen them from all sides, and he no longer knew what to do. Spring came—the time for sowing rye. The farmer's heart sank, because the task was too large for one man and he didn't have the means to hire help.

Quite unexpectedly, one evening three travelers appeared at his door, wind-blown and weary, humbly asking to spend the night. Although they were plainly dressed, these strangers were not ordinary men. In fact, and quite unknown to the farmer, they were three saints—St. Ely, St. George, and St. Nicholas himself!

Detail from the Salvage of the Ship with Grain, *by Fra Angelico, 15th century*

But what does a man give his children if strangers eat his food? "Forgive me," said the farmer, "but I could offer you nothing except a crust of bread. My children are many, and they are very hungry. I wish I could help you, but you must find other shelter."

The stranger who was St. Nicholas replied, "Don't worry! It doesn't matter! I assure you there will be enough bread for your whole family—*and* for us."

Something in the stranger's voice inspired the man to trust him. "Very well," the farmer nodded. "If you agree to stay tomorrow to help sow the rye, I'll let you spend the night."

"We will help," the strangers all promised.

And so it was that the three saints, Ely, George, and Nicholas, stayed at the home of the poor farmer and had supper with his family. The farmer's wife was able to serve only watery soup and small crusts of bread. But as soon as everyone began to eat, the soup turned to a rich, savory stew. And although the guests ate heartily, there was as much bread at the end of the meal as there had been at the beginning, and everyone was well fed. The farmer and his wife looked at one another in surprise.

In the morning, the men went out to sow the rye. George cleared the field of brush and stones. Ely plowed. Nicholas sowed.

On the way back to the farmer's house, Ely said to Nicholas, "Because the poor man let us spend the night, we will see to it that his rye is more beautiful than anyone has ever seen."

"We'll do that, we will," said Nicholas.

That evening, Ely asked the farmer, "Tell me, for whom is it easier: the man at the plow, or the man who sows the seeds?"

"The man at the plow always has it easier," replied the poor man.

Again the farmer's wife served watery soup and a crust of bread for supper, and again the meager fare turned into a fine meal. The strangers ate their fill with the family, bade them farewell, and then went on their way.

While they were walking, Ely said to Nicholas, "I know I promised that the rye will be beautiful, and so it will. But because the farmer said that the man who plows has it easier than the man who sows the seeds, I will see to it that his crop of rye is damaged by hail, so that he gets nothing."

Sure enough, that year the poor man's rye grew more beautiful than anyone had ever seen. He was overjoyed.

Alone, Nicholas went back to the farmer and said, "The priest would like to buy your rye. Be sure to sell it to him; don't keep it."

The farmer still did not know the stranger was St. Nicholas. He knew him only as the traveler who had helped him sow. But again, something in the Saint's voice prompted the man's trust.

By and by, the priest did come to buy the beautiful rye. The poor man sold it to him, just as Nicholas had instructed. But shortly afterward, a tremendous hailstorm flattened the farmer's whole crop.

"Listen," Nicholas said to Ely. "The poor man sold his crop to the priest. It is *his* rye you have destroyed. You have punished the priest, not the farmer!"

"You don't say! Well, if the rye belongs to the priest, I will make it even better than it was!" Ely said.

Without delay, Nicholas hurried to the poor man and said, "When the priest comes and asks for his money back, give it to him."

"But how can I give the money back when hail has destroyed the rye?"

"No matter—just do it."

And so when the priest came asking for his money to be returned, the poor man gave it to him without an argument. Now the rye belonged to the farmer again. And look! Right away, it began to grow beautifully. Soon the crop became even better than it had been before the hail. The poor man was elated. What magnificent rye! Everyone who saw it was amazed.

The rye ripened. Nicholas said to Ely, "The priest requested his money back, and so now the poor man has his rye again—and very beautiful rye it is, too!"

Ely retorted, "It doesn't have to be beautiful. I will take away this advantage so it doesn't help the poor man when the time comes to go to market."

Once more, Nicholas returned to the farmer. "I am, in fact, St. Nicholas, but don't be frightened! I am a simple, modest man. Go to the church and buy my altar a candle for one kopeck. Throw it to the candlestick like you would a bone to a dog; then turn around and leave. For my friend St. Ely, though, buy a very good candle—the best candle you can find. Light it lovingly, and kneel in prayer before it for a long time."

"As you will, Father," agreed the farmer, all the while thinking, "How strange!" But by now he was accustomed to following the Saint's advice. The next Sunday, the poor man went to church and bought two candles—one for St. Nicholas for one kopeck, and one for St. Ely for at least three kopeks. Feeling slightly foolish, he first tossed the candle to the candlestick for Nicholas as if it were a meaty bone for his mutts at home. Then at the altar for Ely, he lit the more expensive candle and prayed and bowed until the sun went down.

The tireless Nicholas returned to Ely, saying, "Look, my good friend, what a disgrace you've brought on me! Obviously, the poor farmer much prefers you! To be sure, he did say that plowing is easier than sowing in the presence of three men, but now he has embarrassed me in front of a whole *church* full of people. He bought me a candle for one kopeck and threw it at the candlestick! But for you he bought a *three*-kopeck candle and placed it nicely. And then he prayed and bowed at your altar until he was exhausted."

"Well and good," shouted Ely, satisfied at last. "For all this piety we will give him a good, full crop of rye!"

That year, the poor man's harvest was greater than he could remember it had ever been. And from then on, he and his family were poor no more.

Ο ΑΓΙΟϹ
ΝΙΚΟΛΑΟϹ

SPANISH FOLKTALE

The Nine Questions

There was once a man and a woman who had a child after longing for one for many years. They were eager to have the baby baptized, but to do so, they needed a godfather. Alas, their friends were too poor to sponsor the newborn. The man searched here and there, but no one was willing.

When the father was about to give up hope, he met an old man who said, "Good morrow to you. Why do you look so sad on such a beautiful day?"

"Ah, me!" said the man, "Why shouldn't I be sad, when I've been looking everywhere for a godfather and cannot find one because I am so poor."

"Don't worry!" said the old man. "I will gladly be the godfather and sponsor the baptism, just as a real godfather should."

"Heaven bless you!" cried the child's parent.

The old man kept his word, and the little one was soon baptized.

Before the godfather returned home, he told the man where he lived and said, "If you ever need anything, just come to me. I will always help you."

"Many thanks, kind sir. But I hardly know you. What is your name?"

The old man said only, "My name is Nicholas." Then he blessed the baby and left.

Saint Nicholas, *Byzantine enamel medallion, 10th century, Madrid*

The father went back to his work at the harbor, anxious to provide for his family. But it was a bad year. The merchants who had hired him said he was no longer needed and sent him away. Soon the man and his wife had spent all of their savings. They had not even enough left to buy flour for bread. In a short time, they and their child would all starve.

Then the poor man suddenly remembered the baby's godfather and his kind offer to help. Right away he went to where Nicholas had said he lived, but the Saint was not at home. After a few days, the man tried again, but again he did not find Nicholas. Many people needed help here and there, and the good Saint must have been busy.

Three times the man made the trip, but Nicholas was still not at home.

Now the man was truly desperate. As he stumbled down the road, weak from hunger, a stranger approached, asking, "My friend, why are you so sad?"

"Why shouldn't I be sad? My wife and child are starving," the man replied.

"Ah, but I can help you!" said the stranger, with a gleam in his eye. "Naturally, though, not for nothing. I propose that we play a game: I will give you this *extremely* large bag of gold, and your troubles will be over. All I ask in return is that you answer my nine questions correctly in a year. If at that time you do not know the answers, then all you must give me is something very small—your child."

"My precious child?" thought the man. "How could I promise that?" His head was spinning, not knowing what to do. But then he thought: "Who knows what will happen in a year? If I don't agree, we'll all starve in a week. It can't get any worse."

"Very well," he said finally. "You have my word on it."

"Good! Smart fellow!" laughed the stranger, and handed him the gold. The happy man hurried home as fast as his weak legs would carry him. That night, he and his family enjoyed a full meal for the first time in many weeks.

With so much gold, the man could have supported his wife and child for much longer than a year. But soon after meeting the stranger, he also found work again. Everything began to go well.

When the year was almost over, though, the man began to worry. He feared for his child whom he had promised to the stranger. "How could I have been so stupid? I don't dare tell my dear wife! Whatever shall I do?" he cried to himself.

But the woman soon noticed that something was amiss. Sorrowfully, he had to tell her the whole story.

"Why don't you go to the godfather of our child? Go to Nicholas!" his wife implored.

"He's never at home," the man sighed.

"Try again!"

Once more the man took the road to where St. Nicholas lived, hardly expecting to find him. But lo and behold! This time, Nicholas was there!

"Now, my friend! How is your child? Is something the matter? Why are you so sad?" St. Nicholas asked.

"Why shouldn't I be sad?" replied the man, and explained everything.

"How foolish!" exclaimed the Saint, "That stranger is none other than a devil. But I'll help you and my godchild. When is the year over?"

The man told him. Nicholas advised him to go home and worry no more.

Precisely one day before the year was up, St. Nicholas appeared at the man's house, saying, "When someone knocks at the door, let me answer it. You must be as quiet as a mouse! Otherwise, you could spoil everything."

Sure enough, just at dusk a year after the man had met the stranger, there was a loud knock on the door. Nicholas raised his hand in caution, and the man and his wife said nothing. Even the baby, awakened by the noise and hungry after a long nap, was silent.

"Who is there?" St. Nicholas asked from behind the door.

"Your lender," came the voice of the devil. "Are you ready to answer my questions?"

"Yes, my friend. Go ahead and ask me!"

"Then tell me, Man, if you can," the devil said, "what is the meaning of the number one?"

"God is one. He is not more or less. My answer's done."

"Good, Man, that's true! Now tell me, What is two?"

"Two are Adam and Eve, ancestors of us all."

"You stand tall!" said the devil. "Now tell me, What is three?"

"Jesus, Joseph, and Marie."

"Man, you know a lot, I do believe. Now tell me, What is four?"

"Matthew, Mark, Luke, and John. Four evangelists and no more."

"Right again! Now tell me, What is five?"

"The five wounds of Christ: two on his hands, two on his feet, and one on his side."

"You *are* a smart fellow!" the devil cried. "But what about the number six?"

"Six points on the bright new star that led to the Babe in the manger."

"You're too smart!" whined the stranger. "But you may not know the number seven!"

"Seven candles in the temple in Jerusalem, by heaven!"

"Well, yes, I must agree. You're no simpleton, I see!" The voice lowered, cold with hate. "Now tell me, What is eight?"

"The number of blessings Christ announced on the mountain."

"Your wisdom is truly a fountain!" sneered the devil. "Until this last question of mine: What is nine?"

"Nine numbers the choirs of angels in heaven. But their songs are not where you belong!" laughed St. Nicholas. "Now, turnabout is fair play. Can you answer a question for me today?"

"Sure, Man! You know a few things, it's true, but I know much more than you. Ask me anything!"

"Tell me, friend, what is thirteen?"

For a moment, there was silence. Then: "Uh, thirteen? I don't know *that*, and neither do you! There is no thirteen." The voice was flat.

"Oh, yes there is, my friend the fiend!" Nicholas chuckled. "You, yourself, are the number thirteen for stirring up trouble, just like a devil. Now disappear and leave my godchild in peace. Otherwise, I'll throw you down to where you deserve to be!"

"ARRRRRGGHHH!" The defeated devil bellowed in rage. Then, in a flash, he was gone.

Hugging the child close, the man and his wife turned to St. Nicholas with tears of gratitude.

"He won't come again." Nicholas assured the couple. "Don't be afraid! And from now on, my good man, I beg you, *do* be more careful about making a deal with a stranger."

And from then on, the good man was more careful, for the rest of his life.

EDITOR'S NOTE: *Since ancient times, thirteen has been considered a number foreboding evil. The Babylonians, for instance, believed thirteen was the number of the Underworld and of the destruction of perfection. The Kabbala refers to thirteen evil spirits, and in the New Testament, it was Judas, the thirteenth guest at the Last Supper, who betrayed Jesus. Groups of twelve-plus-one often occur in folktales: Think of the thirteenth fairy who puts the curse on Sleeping Beauty.*

People are still superstitious about the number thirteen, even today. We have all heard about "Friday the thirteenth." Many hotels skip the number between the twelfth and fourteenth levels because no one would to stay on the thirteenth floor, and many hostesses still do not invite thirteen guests.[6]

But the number thirteen can also be the number for positive change, as it is in this story (and in "The Baker's Dozen" in part 3 of our book). In Greek mythology, the king of the gods, Zeus, was sometimes thought of as the thirteenth in a circle of twelve chief gods. Zeus was famous for bringing about changes in the form of having children, many of whom became important gods and goddesses themselves. In the New Testament, Jesus himself can be thought of as the "thirteenth" in relation to his twelve disciples. And in the fairy tale, how would the prince have ever found Sleeping Beauty, after all, if the thirteenth fairy hadn't put her to sleep?!

UKRANIAN FOLKTALE

The Devil's Wager

In the old days when St. Nicholas still rode his donkey out into the world, it happened that once he met the devil himself.

"Good day, Nicholas," said the devil. "Where are you going?"

"I?" said the Saint. "I am searching here and there. And wherever I find that I am happy, that's where I will stay."

"How boring!" the devil scoffed. "But I have a good idea! Do you know what it is?"

"No, I can't imagine."

"Let's have a little bet! Then the time will pass faster."

"I think time passes just at the right pace, as it is. But very well; I'll wager with you."

The devil said, "Splendid! We will bet. And whoever wins—can eat the other up!"

"Agreed." Nicholas said. "*Bon appetit!*"

"*Merci.* But, uh, what shall we bet about?"

"Well, let's bet . . . that one can guess what the other is thinking," suggested the Saint.

Saint Nicholas on a Donkey, *German, 16th century*

"Yes, it's a deal!"

"Good!" smiled Nicholas. "Now think about something. And I will guess."

The devil closed his eyes tightly. For several moments he was silent except for the tapping of his pointed foot. When he had his idea, he laughed to himself: "I'll get you, you silly saint, because you won't guess it."

Then, pop! His beady eyes opened. He crossed his arms and said smugly, "Well, the time has come. What was I thinking?"

While the devil's eyes were closed, St. Nicholas had been watching him very carefully. He had noticed how the devil's mouth watered and how he smacked his lips. Now Nicholas said lightly, "You were thinking that when you won the bet you would roast me, or perhaps eat me steamed or boiled."

The devil was amazed. "That's right, damn it!" he sputtered. "How did you know that? No matter! Now I will guess what you are thinking!" (And he thought to himself: "Don't worry, he's a saint. It'll be easy to guess what's on his mind!")

Then St. Nicholas closed his eyes. But soon his head drooped, and his long white beard rested on his chest. He had traveled a great distance that day and was almost instantly asleep. A few moments later, he woke up with a start. "Well, well," he mumbled, still in a bit of a daze.

"Aha!" The devil shouted triumphantly. "Now I've caught you! You were thinking about God."

"False," said Nicholas. "I wasn't thinking about anything. My head nodded and I fell asleep."

The devil was so angry, he cried. He wanted to accuse Nicholas of fibbing, but even the devil knew that a saint could hardly lie.

"So!" Nicholas went on, amicably. "You lost this time, but I'll give you another chance. Let's guess what the other has in his hand."

"Yes," said the devil, swallowing his pride, "Let's do that."

"I will begin," said Nicholas. Then the Saint walked around and around, gazing at the ground. Suddenly he leaned forward and moved his arm as if he were lifting a stone. The big sleeve of his robe was in the way, but the devil was paying close attention.

"He can't fool me! He didn't really lift up anything," the devil assured himself. "It will be as it was before—when he had no thought in his head."

At last, Nicholas stood in front of the devil with his hands behind his back. "Now, what do I have in my hand?"

"Nothing at all, you stupid saint!" shouted the devil gleefully, dancing from foot to foot. This time he had surely guessed right.

But when Nicholas had leaned forward, he had pulled a ring from the pocket of his robe. "Look at this!" he smiled, now holding it up for the devil to see. Then he rather pointedly drew it onto his finger.

"WWWWAUGHHH!!!" The devil roared and jumped up and down in anger, but to no avail. He had lost the wager, and the very worst possible had come to pass—he belonged to a saint! Shuddering, he imagined how Nicholas might make a meal of him. Baked? Barbequed? Pickled? His toes curled up at the thought.

As if reading his mind, the Saint laughed. "Poor devil!" he said. "It's enough for me if you will be my servant for a single day. Otherwise, you are free to do what you want."

EDITOR'S NOTE: *And that is how things have been ever since. I wish I could say that the Saint's generosity inspired the devil to change his ways, but the imp keeps company with goodness only on December 6, St. Nicholas Day. A number of people have actually witnessed this phenomenon. I saw it myself last year, on the church square in Prague. There, young and older people alike dressed as St. Nicholas were accompanied by someone else wearing horns.*

WINFRIED WOLF

The Little Nicholas

EDITOR'S NOTE: *Here's a twentieth-century story about a trick that soon got transformed into a happy lesson by a wise parent with a sense of humor.*

One year on December 5, St. Nicholas Eve, the front door suddenly swung wide open. There stood a very small, very young Nicholas in *my* thick winter coat, dragging the bottom half of it on the threshold. My only hat had slipped down over his ears and forehead, so that his eyes just barely peeked out from below. In one hand he was holding a garbage bag; in the other he held an old straw broom.

Wearing my high winter boots that reached almost to his thighs, this little Nicholas clomped up and stood importantly in front of me. "Are you the father of Felix and Clemens?" he asked in a forced deep voice.

Speechless, I could only nod.

"Aha," the little Nicholas bellowed, grabbing an old notebook out of the garbage sack. "Too bad, too bad, but I notice many big sins! For one thing, you don't give your children enough candy! Not only that, you send them to bed too early. And they don't get to watch TV very often. And here's something even worse: You don't play with them enough!"

With Father Christmas's Love, *anonymous, 19th century*

Then with a dramatic flourish the little Nicholas opened up the garbage bag and said: "As a punishment, I'll put you in my sack and carry you away! Get in now!"

Obediently, I climbed in, but the bag only came up to my knees. Now it was the little Nicholas who was speechless. But not for long.

"Well, OK," he said gruffly, "you are lucky enough this time, but you'll get the rod later!"

"No," I shook my head slowly. "I don't think you are the real St. Nicholas."

"Why not?" my little visitor asked, amazed.

"Because the real St. Nicholas doesn't punish. Instead, he praises a person and brings a beautiful present," I answered. "The real St. Nicholas was actually a very good man. He especially loved children and gave them gifts. That's why we have St. Nicholas Day—to remember him."

"But the real St. Nicholas had a rod!" the little Nicholas shouted.

"No," I said, "the real Nicholas was a bishop and always carried his bishop's staff. The rod was invented by fathers and mothers who think their children will obey only when they are afraid."

"And did the real Nicholas have presents for children who *weren't* always so good?" the little one asked.

"Naturally," I answered. "After all, grown-ups aren't always so good, either."

"You're sure?" the little Nicholas insisted. "Is it really true that the children who were sometimes naughty also got a present?"

"Yes," I answered solemnly. "I'm sure that's true."

"That's good!" the little Nicholas shouted with relief. "I'm not the real St. Nicholas, you see. In fact, I'm actually Clemens. But you didn't recognize me, did you?"

"No, I certainly did not! I would never have thought you were Clemens!" I tried to answer with a straight face.

"I didn't think so," cried little Nicholas-Clemens triumphantly. "And I am very good most of the time! Now I'll go find Felix and after that the *real* St. Nicholas will come. Hurrah!"

And with that, eyes bright with anticipation, the little imposter pulled off my hat, kicked off my boots, and bounded up the stairs as fast as he could go with the skirt of my heavy coat trailing behind him.

Detail from Saint Nicholas with Scenes from His Life, *Russian, 16th century*

PART FIVE

Healing Body and Spirit

The Legend of the Healing Myrrh

Then after most blessed Nicholas *had departed from this world to the* Lord, *the tomb in which his venerable corpse was enclosed never ceased to distill an oleaginous liquid, even to this day. To the spot come multitudes of weak, lame, blind, withered, deaf and dumb, and ones who are vexed by unclean spirits. When they are anointed with that holy liquor, they are restored to their original state of health.*

—John the Deacon's *Life of* Nicholas, circa 880 A.D.[7]

As John the Deacon tells us, soon after Bishop Nicholas's death, his followers began to visit his tomb in Myra to pray. These pilgrims soon discovered that even in death their beloved friend had not abandoned them. Nicholas was still with them—*only now, he had genuine miracles to share!* It wasn't long before the people came to regard Nicholas as a saint, for quite regularly, his relics (some say even the rocks of the tomb themselves) would exude a miraculous myrrh—a wonderful, healing liquid or oil. People would anoint themselves with it and soon be healed of their illnesses or injuries.

St. Nicholas Healing a Sick Man, *National Gallery, Budapest*

But more important than physical healing, the oil would also heal the spirit: When pilgrims entered this holy place, those who were troubled in their conscience, saddened by personal tragedy, or simply exhausted from their daily cares would leave it with hearts filled with happiness, peace, and joy. It was as if Nicholas was sharing his own saintly spirit with these ordinary people who loved him.

EDITOR'S NOTE: *There is a long-standing tradition that when evil is present, the oil from the tomb will not flow or refuses to cooperate; but after the evil is corrected, the oil works its healing miracle again.*[8] *We can see evidence of this phenomenon in our later story,* "The Healing Oil."

GREEK FOLKTALE

The Sick King and the Simpleton

EDITOR'S NOTE: *In this folktale, we find a theme common to many fairytales in the motif of the simpleton, sometimes known as the "dumbling." Usually the youngest or third child, and the least valued by his parents at the outset, the simpleton nevertheless proves to have some very special gifts that serve him well in the end.*

There once lived a king who had a wife and three sons. When the boys were almost grown, the king became very ill with leprosy. All of the doctors of the land tried to heal him. But alas, in spite of their remedies, none of them could bring him back to health.

One day an old friend visited him, saying, "I have heard people speak of a very wise man who understands how to heal leprosy. He lives far away in the desert and is not easy to find. But if someone could bring him to you, perhaps he could help."

Filled with new hope, the king summoned his eldest son. "Ride immediately to the desert," he commanded, "and bring back that doctor. Spare no cost!" And he gave his son his best horse and saddlebags filled with gold.

That very morning the eldest son rode away, urging his horse as fast as he could go. The sooner he found the doctor, the sooner he could return to his life

of comfort and ease. But it took him days and days just to reach a city not far from that desert. There he found an inn where he could rest before riding into what looked like endless, barren sand.

As he was sitting at supper, an aged, rather fragile beggar with a long beard appeared at his table. "If you please, sir," he said, "would you give an old man something to eat?"

Annoyed, the son replied, "Why should I, you tiresome fool? Life is not free, you know! If you want something to eat, you must work for me tomorrow. Until then, you'll get nothing!" The old man left without saying a word.

The next morning, the king's son forgot his promise to the beggar. Instead, after asking for directions, he rode away into the desert, whipping his horse to quicken his pace through the deep sand.

Hour after hour he rode under the hot sun, without making any progress. At the top of every dune, all he could see was more sand. At last, his horse stopped, refusing—or unable—to go any further. The king's son was exhausted himself and half-dead of thirst.

"Ah, me," he moaned. "What a miserable way to die."

Just then, suddenly the old man appeared, saying, "Yesterday you refused me. But now I want to give you and your horse something to drink, because at least you had promised me something for today." And he offered water from a leather pouch.

How very sweet that water tasted! The king's son and the horse drank deeply as the old man explained: "The place in the desert where this wise doctor lives is not to be found. Turn around while you still have the strength; you won't reach your goal!" With that, the old man was gone. The son all too gladly took his advice and rode home.

Next the sick king gave his second son the task of bringing back the healer. As he had with his eldest boy, he made sure this one had a good horse and plenty of money.

And so the middle son rode away, pressing his horse to run swiftly, just as his older brother had done. Many days later, he came to the same city and

happened to spend the night in the very same inn, deciding to rest before undertaking the difficult journey into the desert.

Just as the second son was sitting at supper, once again the old bearded beggar came in: "Sir, I'm half starved. Will you please give me a little something to eat?"

Not unkindly, the son answered, "No! The money that bought the food was mine! But wait until I finish my meal. Then you may have what I haven't eaten." And so it was.

The next morning, the king's second son rode forth in order to look for the wonderful doctor in the desert wilderness. But as his older brother before him, he rode hour after hour without finding the hermitage, in spite of urging his horse to go swiftly. Soon he became tired and his horse, weaker.

Through burning eyes, he suddenly saw the old man, who said, "Sir, you are riding in the wrong direction. Turn around! Otherwise, you will collapse in the desert. But because you left me some of your supper, first you and your horse may have something to drink and a few figs."

The king's son already felt he was starving. Gladly he accepted the food and water and shared it with his exhausted horse. Then he, too, hastened to ride home.

"There is nothing we can do. No one can get out of that desert alive!" he swore to his father.

But the youngest son overheard his brother and rushed to the sick king's side, crying, "Please, sir, let me try!"

Now, this youngest son was nothing like his brothers. Where they were practical and perhaps a bit selfish, he was a dreamer and sometimes even seemed to have second sight. But to his father, these qualities made him seem weak.

"No," the king said, "You are too young and inexperienced. You would die where your brothers only barely escaped with their lives."

But the boy, who truly loved his father, begged and begged. His mother, too, implored her husband to let him go, saying, "God will protect and return him safely, whether or not the task can be accomplished."

At last, the king yielded. But he gave this boy, not his finest horse, but a poorer animal, and much less gold than he had given his other two sons, thinking: "My youngest son has little common sense and will spend the money foolishly, like a simpleton."

And so the youngest son rode forth. But because the boy treated the horse kindly and allowed it to stop and rest often, the animal wasn't so poor, after all. Instead, it was very lively and quickly brought the king's son to the same city where his brothers had stayed.

What happened next was as it had been before. As the son was about to begin the evening meal, there at his table was the old man with a beard: "My lord, I am hungry. Do you have a little something for an old man to eat?"

But unlike his brothers, the third son replied amicably, "Yes! Do come and sit with me! There is more than enough for us both." And he offered the old man the very best on his plate and served him a glass of wine, as if he were an old friend.

The next morning, as the king's son was saddling his horse to look for the miracle doctor in the desert, the old man suddenly stood before him, saying, "You were good to me and so I will help you. I am the doctor you seek."

With a flash of insight the boy replied, "Then could you be the healing saint named Nicholas?"

"Yes, I am Nicholas. Look! My donkey is already waiting. Let us ride home to your father. God willing, he will become healthy again."

And so they rode back home to the king.

Before he had even rested, Nicholas examined the sick man. Then he said: "My lord, with God's help I can heal you, but I have one condition."

"Speak!" said the king. "Heal me and you shall receive whatever you wish, if it costs half of my kingdom!"

"No," said the Saint. "I don't want anything for myself. But I insist that your youngest son succeed you as king. I have tested all three of your sons and he is the only one who passed. He is the best man and the one most fit to rule in your place."

At first the king was dumbfounded. But then he touched the old man's hand with his own diseased one and said, "Your wish is strange! But in truth, it was only my youngest son who could do what his brothers could not. I admit I didn't expect that outcome. Very well! If you can make me healthy again, I promise that he will be my successor."

And so it was. Saint Nicholas soon restored the king to health, and then what joy and happiness there was throughout the land! In the fullness of time, the youngest son took his place and ruled the kingdom wisely and well for many long years.

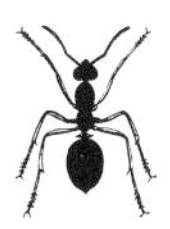

FRENCH FOLKTALE

St. Nicholas and the Ant

EDITOR'S NOTE: *Like another beloved saint,* St. Francis of Assisi, Nicholas *was also widely known as the protector of the very small and weak—including animals, and even insects, as well as children.*

Once there was an ant who was out walking one day, doing what ants do. He didn't notice a little stone in the grass. Before he knew what was happening, he had fallen over it and broken his foot.

Limping on five legs, the ant went to a doctor and said, "Please, could you heal my foot?"

"I would if I could," the doctor replied. "But you know, I can only heal people. Even if I knew how to treat ants, your foot is too little. You must go to a veterinarian instead. There is such a doctor just around the corner."

The ant thanked the doctor and, with much effort, limped around the corner to the veterinarian.

"This is where I broke my foot," the little creature cried, waving the injured appendage in the air. "Could you please help me get well?"

The veterinarian scratched behind his ear and said, "My dear fellow, I only treat mammals. I am not qualified to treat you. Even if I did treat insects, I

A Happy Christmastide, *English Christmas card*

couldn't help you. None of my instruments is precise enough. Your foot is much too small and delicate."

"But what can I do?" exclaimed the ant in distress. "I've already been to the other doctor around the corner. He sent me to you!"

"Yes," the veterinarian said. "I know him, but I really don't know what I can do for you. . . . Wait! I have an idea!"

"What?"

"Go to St. Nicholas!"

"And where does *he* practice?"

"He is just around the other corner in the church."

Now in great pain, the ant dragged himself to the church. He could hardly climb up the steps, but he managed to creep under the door and find his way to where St. Nicholas sat, busy at his desk. With the last strength the ant could muster, he climbed the long way up the Saint's robe and onto the desk.

Right in front of Nicholas's eyes, the ant cried, "Oh, St. Nicholas, please look! I have broken my foot and am in such terrible pain. Can you help me?"

"To be sure," the Saint answered. "Just wait. Your pain will soon stop."

Nicholas barely touched the little creature's foot in the gentlest possible way. In an instant, it was completely healed.

"Thank you! Thank you!" shouted the ant. Then on all six of his sprightly little legs, he skipped off the desk, jumped down the Saint's robe, and ran the whole way home.

ARMENIAN FOLKTALE

The Hermit and the Mouse Maiden

EDITOR'S NOTE: *Here is another story celebrating* Nicholas *as the protector of the very small!*

Before Nicholas became the Bishop of Myra, he was a hermit in the desert, living in a cave for many years. As always, he was very modest in his needs. Sometimes pious people brought him herbs and bread, and when they did, he was careful not to waste anything. The desert was so desolate and lonely that even the wild animals had a hard time surviving there.

One day as Nicholas was praying, a little mouse who had lost her way chanced to find him. Seeing how hungry she was, Nicholas scattered some of the bread he had been given on the ground for her. At first the frightened mouse ran back a distance. But the man did not move, and soon the tiny creature was sitting up on her hind legs, wriggling her nose as she sniffed the scent of the food.

Then . . . Ki-TEEK, Ki-TEEK, Ki-TEEK! She streaked forward and carried the bread away to safety. Oh, my! How very good it tasted!

And so it was. Every day Nicholas would leave bread for the mouse, and every day she would come to eat it. Before long, she became accustomed to the man, and the lonely hermit grew accustomed to having her near.

Nicholas even tried to communicate with the mouse, watching closely as she listened and nodded her head. At last, he thought, "I have found someone in the desert to talk with. Praise God for this gift!"

One day, Nicholas realized to his amazement that he could understand the mouse's language.

"If I were a human being," the little creature said, "I would go to the village to find a young man to marry."

"Perhaps that would be possible, perhaps not," her friend replied. "I'll ask God to help and we'll see what happens." Then Nicholas prayed from deep within.

When he awoke the next morning, in the corner of his cave where the mouse usually sat, there was a young woman! And a pretty young woman she was, too. There was nothing mousy about her at all.

Nicholas said to her, "Now you see what can be done, by God's grace. And now perhaps your dream can come true. I, myself, will take you to the next village. There we shall soon see."

So, for the first time in many years, Nicholas left his hermitage in the desert. And because the girl was very pretty, in the village they found many admirers. Nicholas would have preferred she marry a good older man, but, as happens everywhere, the girl had her own thoughts and wishes and fell in love with a young man.

"So be it!" agreed Nicholas, entrusting the girl to the young man's care. Then he returned to his cave in the desert.

The marriage of the mouse-girl and the young man went as marriages often do: In the beginning, both were very much in love and happy. But when the novelty wore off, the young man began to complain that his wife had not brought any dowry to the marriage. Soon afterward, he began to beat her and demand she do heavy work beyond her strength. With every hour that passed, the mouse-girl's heart grew heavier still.

At last, one day it was too much for the young woman. She waited until her husband had left the house, and then—Ki-TEEK, Ki-TEEK, Ki-TEEK—she ran as fast as she could back to Nicholas in the desert.

When he saw her, he said sadly, "What should we do now? You can't marry any other man, and you can't stay with me."

"Pray to God that he turns me back into a mouse," she said.

"Yes, I can try that. But what then? Who knows?"

All day and long into the evening, Nicholas prayed intensely. When he awoke the next morning—there sat the mouse in the corner!

"God be praised!" he exclaimed. "Now what should we do?"

"My dear friend, put me in your sack and carry me to where there are many mice. There I'll find a proper husband."

And that's just what Nicholas did: He took her to a deep ravine in the desert where he knew there would be many mice living in the dense sage along the banks of a small creek. Gently he lifted the mouse from his sack and looked into her bright black eyes. Gently she brushed his cheek with her whiskers. Then he set her down on the desert floor.

"Farewell, dear one," she said. "I will never forget you."

"Nor I, you!" he replied. "Blessed be they who know themselves."

Then Ki-TEEK, Ki-TEEK, Ki-TEEK—the little mouse scampered off to the safety of the sage.

Nicholas returned to his desert cave and remained there until the people of Myra called him to become the Bishop. In the meantime, we trust that the mouse found a good husband and lived happily for many years to come.

Ki-TEEK, Ki-TEEK, Ki-TEEK!

KARELIAN FOLKTALE

St. Nicholas and the Monster

EDITOR'S NOTE: *This is a spooky tale that could be told dramatically on* All Saint's Day *as well as at any other time of the year. We've added the little refrains to make the story more fun for children, who love such chanting rhymes. You could also invent nine other tasks for the monster, if you're feeling inspired!*

In a little town on the other side of the lakes and the forests lived a very wicked man. Violent and greedy, hard-hearted and full of lies, he was—in short—a kind of monster. He refused to do any honest work. Instead, he made a fortune by finding ways to betray those who trusted him, cheat his associates, and steal from those who had less than he did.

But in the end, what is the advantage of being rich, if one's spirit is impoverished? We must all die, and no amount of bargaining will buy a few additional hours.

And so it was in God's time that the wicked thief himself died and was laid in his coffin. The decent townsfolk carried him into the church and even sang a Mass for him. They wanted to carry him to the cemetery and bury him. But try

St. Nicholas of Bari, *by* Jacopo Robusti Tintoretto, *16th century*

as they would, and even though the air was not cold, the coffin was frozen stiff and could not be moved.

What to do? The people tried incense and holy water, but to no avail. The priest hastily crossed himself and reported everything to the bishop. Soon afterward, the bishop arrived and acted with some ceremony, but even he was helpless: In spite of every effort, the coffin couldn't be moved.

Crossing himself in turn, the bishop sent for his most devout monks. All day long they prayed over the coffin, and they would have done so through the dark hours as well. But at midnight, just as the church tower bell tolled for the twelfth time, the monster climbed out of his box, rolling his wild eyes and wagging his tongue hideously. FFFWWWAMP! He tried to grab one of them, who barely got away! Then they all fled—townsfolk, clergy, and bishop alike.

Now no one wanted to go back into the church. The closest they would come was to make a big circle around the building. But their prayers and songs had no effect there, either.

At last, the people went to the lord of the land for help. His solution was to offer a reward, promising to pay whoever could drive out the dead man as much gold as it had cost to build the church.

How generous! Well and good! But who would take up the challenge? People still gave the church wide berth as they walked down the street. Nobody dared to go in. Since the monster had been so evil in life, how much more evil might he be as a dead man!

When evil actions take the lead,
Friend and foe are full of need.

Just on the outskirts of town, there lived a poor widow with a single son. One day the young man said to his mother, "Let me go to the church!"

"Absolutely not, my son," she answered, "The monster will eat you up."

But the boy was as headstrong as he was brave. "No, Mother!" he argued. "God willing and with the help of His saints, I'll drive out that disgraceful fellow."

What could the woman do in the face of such reverent determination? Needless to say, she let him go.

On the way, her son met an old man who asked kindly, "Where are you going, my boy?"

"Sir," the son replied, "I am going to drive the monster out of the church, so the people can pray there again safely."

"Good," said the old man. "I'll help you."

"That's very kind of you, I'm sure," said the boy respectfully, "but to cope with *this* danger requires great strength. The only help we could use would be that of a saint, such as Nicholas."

The old man smiled. "Don't worry, my boy. I'm familiar with such things and have found help from heaven many times."

And so the two of them arrived at the church together. There lay the monster, as still as a stone. The old man lit candles all around the coffin. Then he stood at the head, the boy stood at the foot, and they began to sing and pray. Evening came; the light faded through the stained glass windows into night. Still the old man and the boy sang and prayed. At last, the bell in the tower tolled midnight. Just at the stroke of twelve, the monster rose up out of the coffin, and out of his wide, cruel mouth came a terrible roar. The boy began to run away, but the old man cried, "Wait! Don't be afraid. I can manage him!"

Side by side they approached the monster, his powerful arms flailing the air. But somehow, the creature soon realized what the youth did not know. . . .

To the boy's amazement, the brute lowered his arms and just stood there, glaring at them. The youth was even more amazed when the old man grabbed the monster by his collar and said, "During your life you were an evil person. But your mother in heaven has been praying for you, and so Our Lord God is going to allow a time of grace. If you will serve me and the poor for twelve years, you will also go to heaven. Follow me."

To the bewildered boy, the old man said, "Don't be afraid, and stay in the church until morning. Nothing will happen to you. Then you will get a reward for your courage and be able to take good care of your mother."

"Yes, sir, but who *are* you?" exclaimed the boy.

The monster croaked a dry laugh. "Don't you recognize St. Nicholas? Not even I can make mischief with him!"

The boy's eyes widened in wonder as the Saint smiled at him and then firmly led the monster out of the church. When they came to a creek, Nicholas said, "Wash yourself here. Your face is filthy, and you might frighten people."

After the monster obeyed, he didn't look so strange. Now he seemed just like any other rather rough-tough man—maybe even better than he had looked in life! For three days, he followed the Saint through the deep forests on the other side of the lake. Then they came to a river, and Nicholas led the man to a hut where there was a small boat.

"The ferryman has just died," the Saint told him. "Your first job is to transport the people who come here to the other shore. You must not charge the poor people anything, but you may ask the rich for a small price. After all, you'll need some money to buy food to eat. In a year, I will return and lead you to another kind of work."

And so it was. The rough man, once an evil monster, now became a ferryman. In the beginning, he didn't like the hard work and was very moody. But after he had taken many poor people to the other shore and received such warm thanks because he didn't ask for money, he felt some warmth around his heart. "What an awful man I was!" he thought, regretting his earlier life.

One good deed for bad to show—
Now eleven left to go!

Exactly one year later, St. Nicholas returned and brought another ferryman. (Who knows what *he* had done!) Then he took the first one to a poor farmer's family where he had to work all day just to earn his food.

At first, the rough-tough man hated this work, too. But soon he began to enjoy the birds singing at dawn, the scent of the wild flowers along the path, the warm sun on his back as he plowed the field, and his sense of accomplishment at the end of the day. What's more, now he wasn't alone any more. He learned how hard life is for poor people; but because the farmer's family was friendly to him, he also learned the pleasure of being liked. He began to like *himself*, and he became a very industrious worker.

Two good deeds for bad to show—
Now just ten are left to go!

Once again, after one year St. Nicholas returned. This time, he took the former monster to a woman whose husband, a fisherman, had drowned in a storm. Now the fellow was told he must take the fisherman's place and provide for the widow's large family. By this time, the man *wanted* to do the right thing, but he was afraid he couldn't live up to the task. He did, though, just as he was supposed to do. Not only did he care well for the woman and her many children, but he also felt the comfort of companionship for the first time.

Three good deeds for bad to show—
Now just nine are left to go!

The years passed. Who knows what other tasks the man had to accomplish until the twelve years were up! Whatever they were, in God's own time the former monster became a good man and was completely changed.

When Nicholas came for the twelfth time, he said, "The first time around you made only trouble, but now your spirit is healed and you have made peace. The rest of your reparation I will leave up to the Lord God Himself. Now come with me to your mother in Paradise."

And so it happened—not at the stroke of midnight, but just at the dawn of a beautiful new day.

When evil actions take the lead,
Friend and foe are full of need.
But when bad deeds are turned to good,
Things come 'round as they should!

ARMENIAN FOLKTALE

The Healing Oil

EDITOR'S NOTE: *The motif of the healing oil has its roots in the tradition described by John the Deacon at the beginning of* "The Legend of the Healing Myrrh." *One could ask oneself*—What is *the healing oil?* Perhaps *it is a symbol.*

Once upon a time, a long time ago, there was a young man who could not find good work in his own country, so he left home to try his luck in a distant land. He was industrious and thrifty and soon prospered. In a very short time, he had made a small fortune. But one day, he yearned to be with his family and friends again, so he packed his belongings and set forth to go home.

The journey was long and difficult and led across a range of mountains. As he was climbing up a narrow path, suddenly the young man saw an old man almost collapsing under the weight of a heavy sack. The young man approached him and said compassionately, "Dear grandfather, may I help you?"

"Oh, God, yes, please!" the old fellow answered. "I don't think I could carry this sack a moment longer."

"Give it to me," offered the youth. "I'm accustomed to heavy loads, and it would give me pleasure to help you." He slung the sack over his shoulders as

---

Scenes from the Life of St. Nicholas, *by Herman Rode, 15th century*

easily as if it were filled with goose down, saying, "You lead the way, since I don't know where you are going."

For many hours, the two of them trudged along over the steep and stony path. It was evening by the time they reached the top of the mountain, where there was a little house and a small chapel.

"Here we are, at last!" the old man said. "Put down your heavy load and let's see if we can still find something to eat in the house."

"Dear grandfather," the boy replied, "that won't be necessary. I have food—more than enough for two—and there's even some wine."

"Yes, but I cannot pay you, my boy!"

"Who said anything about paying? You are my companion on the way; what belongs to me belongs to you."

And so it was. The two men entered the hut, lit a fire against the night chill, and ate. Then, exhausted but refreshed, they lay down to sleep.

The next morning, the young fellow said, "Dear grandfather, can I help you with anything? Just tell me and I will gladly do it!"

"No," the old man answered. "You've already done more than enough. And for your trouble, I want to give you a small gift."

From his sack he produced a little bag drawn at the top with a thong. "Look! In this goat pouch is oil. It seems small and shabby, but the oil inside is no common oil. Not only does it smell good, it is healing. When you anoint the sick or wounded with *this* oil, they will soon be well again."

The young man shook his head, saying he needed no payment. But the old man urged him, "You gave without asking for anything in return. Now you should receive in the same spirit. That way, you can continue to be of help, and you yourself will benefit—you'll see!"

The old man may have been weak, but there was nothing weak about his opinions! (Unbeknownst to his young friend, he was, in fact, none other than St. Nicholas himself.) The boy accepted the goat pouch with many thanks, bade his companion farewell, and then walked on down the far side of the mountain into the valley.

The first village he came to had been devastated by a gang of thieves. They had murdered almost all the people and left others half-dead. The few who were unharmed were mourning for their loved ones, even while they were happy to be alive themselves. The young man was deeply saddened at the sight of such grief and suffering.

"Now!" he said to himself. "We shall see whether the old man's oil can really help."

Going from house to house, he treated each victim with a little of the sweet-scented oil. And lo and behold! As from a long sleep, the people began to stir. Their eyes opened, clear of pain, and the color returned to their cheeks. One by one, wounds closed and bones mended. Soon each patient was standing and quite well again.

Joyfully, the villagers offered gifts to the youth with the miraculous healing oil. But he refused, saying, "I have received without paying, and I will give without payment. Something to eat and drink in your good company I will gladly take. Nothing more."

That night, what a feast there was in the village! What music they made! The next morning, the young man left the people with some of the marvelous oil and then continued on his way.

When he arrived in the next village, he found it too had been overrun by bandits. There were more inhabitants here than at the first village, and so the number of injured was greater, too. Only the few who had been able to hide during the attack were left unharmed. For days, the young man worked from sunrise to sunset tending the wounded. Finally, all had been healed and he was able to leave.

Everywhere he traveled, the news spread quickly before him: A young man is coming who knows how to cure the sick! He has an especially wonderful healing oil!

And so there was always plenty for the young man to do. What surprised him was that the oil never ran out, although he had already treated so many and had even given a little of it away now and again. But the "shabby" little goat pouch was still as full as it had been on the day he received it from the old man (whom *we* know was St. Nicholas).

Late one evening, the young fellow came to a secluded house where a single monk lived all alone. Cold and tired, the young man knocked on the door and asked for a place to sleep. When the monk waved him inside, the young man noticed that his hand was injured and said, "That looks painful, Brother. Allow me to treat it for you."

"Aha!" thought the monk. "This must be the fellow with the miracle pouch."

Sure enough, of course, the young man drew out the bag. He rubbed a little of the soothing oil on the monk's hand, and it healed in an instant. Smiling broadly, the monk offered the fellow food and drink and a warm bed by the fire. As soon as the young man fell asleep, the monk exchanged his pouch for another one that looked just the same. "What you can do, I can do also, my friend!" he thought to himself. "One must be clever in this world!"

The next morning, the young man didn't notice that the pouch had been exchanged. Nor did he notice anything odd about the milk he drank—into which the monk had secretly poured some opium. After his breakfast, the youth thanked the monk for his hospitality and set forth briskly on his way. But he soon became so tired that he sat down at the edge of the path and fell into a deep sleep.

The crafty monk had been following him at a distance, waiting for this moment. Chuckling quietly, he left the young fellow by the side of the path and walked on to the next village, where he presented *himself* as the miracle healer.

The people looked at each other in surprise. Hadn't they been hearing about a *young* man? This fellow already had gray hair! Still, they were more hopeful than suspicious. The monk waited until a large number of sick people had gathered. Then he began collecting money, saying, "Nothing is given for nothing. If it's not expensive, it has no value."

Now the people became distrustful, indeed. Hadn't they heard that the young healer asked for nothing in return? Nevertheless, some threw a gold coin into the monk's cap. Others held back, thinking, "Let's wait and see . . ."

The first to pay was a woman who sat down heavily and stretched out her lame foot. The monk, with a grandiose gesture, pulled out the little pouch and poured from it into his hand. But what was this? Out of the pouch came, not sweet-scented oil, but a stinking brew—as black and as thick as tar. And when the monk applied it to the woman's foot, she cried, "Oh! You are hurting me! And what is that awful stench?"

The monk answered smoothly, "I beg your pardon! I forgot to shake the pouch and so the oil was not properly mixed! But I'll do it now, and all will be well. Let the next patient come!"

He began to swing the pouch up and down and all around. Then with a flourish, he rubbed its oil onto his next paying customer—a rich merchant with an infected boil on his cheek. But now the stuff smelled even worse, and it was so sticky the poor man could not wipe it from his face. Boxing the monk's ears, he bellowed, "You are a charlatan. Give me my money back!"

A tumult broke out. The villagers beat the monk soundly and threw his pouch on a pile of manure, shouting that now it had found its true home.

Limping and bruised, the monk dragged himself away. That night, St. Nicholas appeared to him and said sternly, "You criminal! What have you done? You have betrayed the people and stolen money! Is this the work of a holy man? You will have to pay for your actions and suffer!"

"Yes!" cried the monk. "Now I see that I have been wrong, and I regret everything. But I want to make amends. I will pray for forgiveness, and in the future, I will help people without asking for anything."

Nicholas's tone softened slightly. "Very well. If you do as you promise, you will be forgiven. If not, you'll have more trouble than you can imagine. You'll be like the thick tar in that bag of yours, only you'll smell worse! I ask no payment for this advice, dear monk, but its value is great. A wise man would heed it well!"

Humbled, the monk limped home. Did he keep his promise? Perhaps, perhaps not. If he didn't, it wasn't for lack of understanding.

But let's leave him to his fate and return to the young man—who, after recovering from the monk's opium, continued on his way. Soon he arrived at the village where the monk had been the day before. There, perched on a pile of manure, was the young man's pouch. He swooped it up and left the monk's bag in its place.

Then he began offering to heal those in need. Naturally, at first the people were distrustful. They weren't about to be fooled by another fraud! Even though this man seemed sincere, they didn't believe him.

But unlike the monk, this young man asked for nothing but to help. He didn't ask for money. Soon people were saying to themselves, "It won't cost anything to let him try. What is there to lose? If he's lying, we'll beat him up!"

What happened next put all their doubts to rest. The oil the young man produced had a most delightful fragrance, like that of Lebanese incense, or an expensive smelling-water used by elegant ladies. Suddenly the air was perfumed with the scent of carnations, or perhaps jasmine, or lavender. . . .

And everyone the young man treated realized within moments that their wounds were healed and their broken limbs were whole again. More and more people began to gather for a drop of the wonderful oil from the little goat pouch.

Soon the rumor of a miracle doctor reached the palace of the prince. As it so happened, this prince had long suffered from leprosy. His body was wasted with fever and covered with painful sores. The best doctors in the land had not been able to cure him. When the prince heard the story of the healing oil, he sent his messenger to bring the young man at once.

Politely but firmly, the young man replied, "Tell the prince I will come tomorrow. Today I have so many other suffering patients that I cannot get away."

At first the prince was angry and impatient. But then he realized, "This is an honest man. He seeks neither money nor honor. Such a man would be just the right sort to have in our country!"

The next morning, the young man arrived as promised and was soon led into the presence of the sick prince. Not without dignity in spite of his condition, the prince said, "If you can heal me, I will give you half my kingdom and the hand of my daughter in marriage. If you do not, I will imprison you for betraying me."

With equal dignity, the young man replied, "My prince, I do not need your kingdom. As for your daughter—whoever becomes her husband, she should decide for herself. But if the Lord God is with me, you will quickly be healed."

Then once again he poured some drops of the precious healing oil onto his hands. As he salved the prince's sores, they began to shrink and shrivel away. Within moments, the sick man's skin was smooth and flush with health, and his fever was completely gone. That day and for many more, bells of rejoicing rang throughout the land, thanks to St. Nicholas!

As for the rest, whether the young man married the prince's daughter, who knows? Perhaps, perhaps not. But it is certain that his eyes were as kind as hers, and that his touch was as gentle as it was healing. Being a bright young woman, she would probably have chosen him.

It is also certain that somewhere, a small bottle of the miraculous healing oil still remains. But where could it be? Ah! That is for you to discover, dear reader. Go and find it!

SWEDISH FOLKTALE

Holy Night

EDITOR'S NOTE: *With this lovely tale, we move on from stories about* St. Nicholas *to the coming of* Christmas *itself, with all its mystery and healing power.* (*By the way, in this story we also find another curious example of a folktale being introduced in the first person.*)

My grandfather used to tell us this story when we children were full of restless excitement about the coming holidays. His deep, low voice soon filled us with silent wonder:

Long, long ago there was a doctor who lived far away in the north of Sweden. Although he took care of everyone throughout a large region, he never seemed to tire. On the contrary, he was always accommodating and friendly, and he was particularly good with children. He had a beautiful home at the edge of a small village, where, being unmarried, he lived only with an older housekeeper and his coachman.

No other doctor was available far and wide, so this one was very, very busy. In the summer, he traveled by coach to visit his patients; in the winter, he went by sleigh. Because the area had no drug store, he also maintained his own pharmacy.

One year, the winter was extremely hard. The rivers had frozen early and

Detail of the Christ Child from the Madonna delle Ombre (*Madonna of the Shadows*), *by Fra Angelico, 15th century*

the heavy snow kept falling until the mountain roads were entirely blocked. The doctor could only take care of patients who lived in the lowlands, since the mountains and the forests were closed to travelers. If he dared to leave the village, he and his coachman took their rifles, because the cold and hunger had driven the wolves and bears out of their caves. Even in daylight, the desperate animals were coming too close for comfort.

On the other side of the mountains was a tiny village, where there lived a farmer whose little girl was extremely ill. She had been weakened by a high fever for many days. Her mother had tried everything. Nothing seemed to help; the child's fever was still rising.

"You must ride to the doctor without delay," the woman told her husband. "Otherwise, our daughter will surely die."

The farmer sadly shook his head. "It is just not possible," he replied. "You know I would do anything to help our child, but the forests are completely snowed in. And even if I could get through on horseback, how could the doctor come with his sleigh? We can only wait and hope for the best."

But his wife kept pressing her husband, arguing that he could at least bring back some of the doctor's good medicine.

At last, the farmer saddled his horse, took his rifle, and began the ride to the next village. But he had hardly reached the edge of the forest when his horse sank knee-deep in the snow. Within moments, a pack of wolves surrounded him with their long fangs. In his frantic eagerness to turn around, his horse fell. Only by firing the gun could the man get back to his house safely, for the wolves pursued him to the very entrance of his farmyard.

"I can't do it!" he cried, bursting through the door. "The snow is too deep! And the wolves are vicious! Besides, it is getting dark. God bless our child!" In utter discouragement, he led his bleeding horse back to its stall.

Weeping, his wife returned to the room where their feverish daughter lay.

"Mother, why are you crying?" the child asked.

"Oh, your father has just come home," her mother answered, trying to compose herself. "He wanted to get medicine from the doctor, but he can't because there is so much snow. But he'll try again soon!"

"Don't worry, Mother! If you feel we need the doctor, I'll tell the Christ Child when he comes. That's what you told me this morning, isn't it—that tonight the Christ Child will come?"

"Yes, dear, but that is an old saying, meant to remind us that Jesus came into this world as a child."

"No," the little girl insisted weakly. "I am certain that if I pray for it, the Christ Child himself will come to help me."

Her mother said nothing, but kissed the girl on her hot forehead and left the room. To her husband, she said: "Our child's fever is worse again."

Later, the woman prepared their Christmas Eve dinner with a joyless heart, thinking, "This will be our daughter's last Christmas."

Every now and then she tiptoed to the girl's room and looked in. One time, cheeks flaming, the little one cried, "Oh, Mother! The Christ Child was just here! He looks like a little boy. I told him he should send for the doctor. He promised to go right away!"

The child was so excited that her mother called her father, and they heard the whole story again. "Her fever must be higher," the father thought. "She's imagining things now." But the mother began to hope.

Christmas Eve came to the doctor's village with its mystery and its magic. Everywhere, families gathered together. Only the doctor was alone, for his housekeeper and coachman had gone to be with their relatives. The good physician was preparing some medicine, when someone knocked at the door.

"Come in," he called. To his surprise, when the door swung open, there stood a little boy, who took off his hat and greeted him warmly. His coat was covered with snow, and his cheeks were red from the cold.

"Who are you, my child?" the doctor asked. "I thought I knew all the children around here, but you I've never seen before."

"I only come at Christmas," the boy said simply. "They sent me from the village on the other side of the mountain because they need your help."

The doctor raised his brow. "You little trickster! Do you think I don't know how much snow there is?" he laughed. "And do you really expect me to believe that people would send such a young boy to fetch me? The bears and the wolves would have torn you apart as soon as you stepped into the forest."

"No," said the boy, his eyes bright. "I am quite serious. I have a sister who is very ill and needs your help. You yourself say you don't know me. If you don't come, the girl will die!"

The doctor's voice grew soft. "My dear boy, even if you were right, I couldn't help you. My coachman is with his family tonight and I couldn't take him away. Besides, he wouldn't drive in the forest after dark under any circumstances."

"That isn't necessary. I have my own sleigh. I can drive you and bring you back home again, as well."

"But the wild animals would eat us!" exclaimed the doctor, now quite upset. "Only our boots and buttons would be left."

"Don't you know this is Christmas Eve?" insisted the boy. "Wild animals won't hurt anyone tonight."

"You are a dear child," the doctor said, "but what you are telling me is only a pious legend. The animals know nothing of the calendar! I would gladly help your sister, but it is too risky."

The boy's eyes grew deep and serious. "Are you afraid?" he asked gently.

"Yes."

"Don't you trust God?"

The doctor considered and then answered, "You are right! It should be as God wills. I don't want to be put to shame. Wait a moment! I'll get my bag and my rifle, and then we'll go. I hope you have a strong horse."

"You'll see! Leave your rifle at home. We won't need it."

But the doctor thought, "Better to be safe." He gathered his gun along with his medicine bag and then announced, "We can go now."

Outside the house, sure enough, there was the sleigh and its lantern. When he saw the "horse," the doctor rubbed his eyes and looked again. It was a very, very big animal and carried enormous antlers—in fact, it was an elk.

"I must say, you have a strange horse!"

"The best you could have for this weather," the child replied with a smile. He helped the doctor into the sleigh and carefully covered him with warm blankets. Then he scrambled up onto the driver's bench and whistled to the elk, whose gigantic steps pulled the sleigh as if it were as light as a feather. In no time, they were out of the village and approaching the forest. By the light of the pale moon, suddenly the doctor saw the gleaming eyes of the wolves and reached for his rifle.

That very moment, the boy turned and said, "Please put your gun down! You don't understand how to travel among the animals. I will teach you."

The man did as the child told him, thinking, "From the mouth of babes! This boy is more capable than you are yourself."

Then he listened in awe as the boy called to the wolves. They seemed to understand him and made no move to attack. Quite the opposite! Instead, some of them ran in front of the sleigh and stamped down the snow while others ran behind, as if to protect the riders. Curiously, the wolves didn't disturb the elk at all. He made his way quite easily through the forest, even where it was not possible to run so fast. The sleigh never got stuck, and they reached the farmer's little settlement sooner than expected.

"Here's the house," said the boy, "Quickly! Let's go inside to my sister."

The boy helped the doctor with his bag out of the sleigh, and the good man knocked on the door. As you can imagine, the parents could not have been more startled to see him.

"How did you get here? How did you know our daughter is sick?!"

"It's a surprise to me as well," responded the doctor. "Your son came to get me. And I must say, a very capable lad he is! You must be proud of him. And you must have great faith in God to let him travel alone among the hungry wolves through the winter forest."

"What did you say? Excuse me, but there must be some mistake!" the father said. "I have no son. Our daughter is our only child."

"But the boy said he came to get me for his sick sister. How confusing! And how did you ever train that big elk to pull the sleigh?"

"What elk?" Now the farmer, too, was mystified. The doctor led him outside to see for himself. There indeed was the sleigh with its unusual draft animal, but the boy had disappeared.

"What a strange reindeer!" cried the farmer. "It doesn't belong to me or anyone else in our village."

"We'll think about it later! Take me to your daughter."

When the parents ushered the doctor into the sick room, the girl sat straight up in bed and said, "Mama, the Christ Child was here again. He said that I will soon be well, and that I should tell the doctor he is sorry he doesn't have time to take him home, but that the elk can find the way and the doctor shouldn't be frightened."

The grown-ups all looked at each other pointedly. "This is a strange story!" exclaimed the doctor.

"Yes," said the father sorrowfully. "It comes from the fever."

"No, something quite different is involved here." And to the girl the doctor said, "Don't worry. When you have this kind of friend, you will surely get well."

He gave her a strong medicine. Then he sat down with her parents for a fine Christmas Eve dinner, gladly accepting their invitation to spend the night.

The next morning, to the parents' great joy, the girl's fever was completely gone! In his happiness, the father ran outside and soon brought back a beautifully shaped little pine tree that he stood upright in the girl's room. Her parents had been too worried to decorate for the holiday before. Now the girl's eyes shined as the sweet, fresh piney scent filled the air.

After satisfying himself that all was well, the doctor prepared to leave. "What will the trip be like this time?" he asked himself curiously.

Sweden is so far to the north that even though the winter sun had just risen in the sky, it was already late in the day when the father escorted the doctor out of the house.

"I can't believe it—it *is* an elk!" the farmer shouted. "Yesterday I thought it was just a reindeer."

And with that, the two men laughed and bade each other farewell.

The trees were already casting long shadows as the elk pulled the doctor's sleigh through the forest. The man shuddered with fear, wishing with all his heart that the boy from the previous evening were there now.

Sure enough, around a bend on the path, a pack of wolves was waiting! Quickly the doctor raised his rifle, but the elk turned his majestic head and said, "Put that gun down! They won't harm us."

"Now I must have the fever!" the frightened man said to himself. "I could swear I just heard that animal talk!"

Onward the elk pulled the sleigh until it reached the wolf pack. Then the doctor heard the lead wolf say, "This is the man the boy from heaven brought and said we should lead back to his home."

The elk nodded, and the pack began running, some ahead, and some behind the sleigh. At first everything went well, but at a steep slope the sleigh tipped over and the doctor fell out. Before the doctor had even begun to shiver, a bear came running up and lifted him gently out of the snow and back into the sleigh, which the wolves had set upright again.

"Are you hurt?" the bear asked, brushing the snow off the man's coat.

"No, not at all, thank you," answered the doctor, calmly arranging his blankets. He was now beyond being surprised at anything.

The wolves and the bear stayed protectively near as the sleigh traveled through the forest to the other side of the mountain. Then the wild animals said farewell except for the elk, who took the doctor all the way home.

Ever since then, the people of that region have often whispered to one another, "Our doctor has become a little strange." It is an observation with which, if the good man heard it, he would certainly agree.

On more than one occasion, his friends and neighbors have observed him talking with the bears and the wolves. They have noticed, too, that the animals never harm him, so that he is able to visit his patients without danger all year long. What's more, sometimes, especially in the winter twilight, his horse looks huge and seems to have antlers as it easily pulls the doctor's sleigh through the deep snow in the forest.

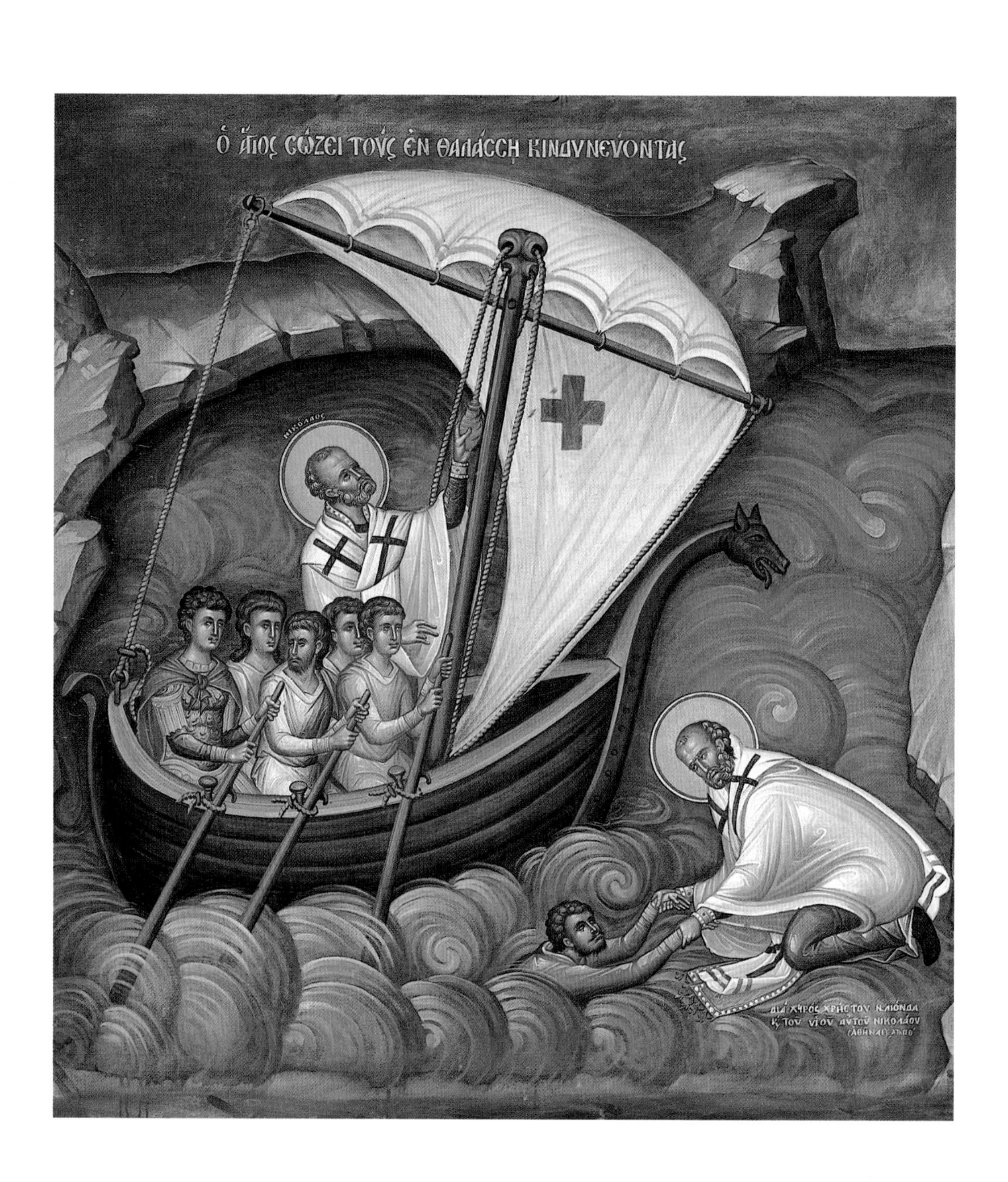
Ο ΑΓΙΟΣ ΣΩΖΕΙ ΤΟΥΣ ΕΝ ΘΑΛΑΣΣΗ ΚΙΝΔΥΝΕΥΟΝΤΑΣ
ΝΙΚΟΛΑΟΣ
ΔΙΑ ΧΕΙΡΟΣ ΧΡΗΣΤΟΥ Ν. ΛΙΟΝΔΑ
Κ ΤΟΥ ΥΙΟΥ ΑΥΤΟΥ ΝΙΚΟΛΑΟΥ
(ΑΘΗΝΑΙ)

Signs of St. Nicholas Today

In March 2000, some friends and I were visiting Greece to research material for this book. The spirit of St. Nicholas is very much alive in Greece to this day, particularly in Crete. We spoke with many people who have had or have heard first-hand accounts of the Saint's helpful intervention. These are not documented medical cases, but they are real reports, nonetheless. Here are a few of them:

A MODERN LEGEND OF RESCUE AT SEA

It was a balmy evening in the bustling Greek town of Heraklion, the capital city on the island of Crete. We had just settled down for dinner in a restaurant owned by a local friend, Panagiotis Milonakis. It was only about seven o'clock, early for dinner in Greece. We were anticipating good conversation and hoping for a story.

We were not to be disappointed. Without being in the least self-conscious, tall and very manly, Panagiotis began talking about his grandfather, now deceased. He had the greatest respect for this grandfather and spoke with many hand gestures and a voice full of reverence, as translated by my companions Mia Dallas and Ed Tick:

Saint Nicholas Rescuing Sailors. *Contemporary icon handpainted by Christos N. Liondas, Athens, Greece*

This is a true story my grandfather told me some twenty years—no—now about *forty* years ago. Like all the men in my family, my grandfather loved to fish. One day, in good weather, he and several others went out in our forty-foot fishing boat. It was a calm, quiet, sunny day, but before they fully realized what was happening, a terrible wind arose. In no time, the boat began to rock and reel in the pounding waves.

The storm rapidly grew worse and worse. The howling wind became more treacherous. The men covered everything they could to keep the water out of the ship, but it began to list badly out of control. The storm had become a tempest with terrible power, and they all expected to die soon.

Desperately, they knelt in prayer—first to God, then to the Virgin Mary, and finally to St. Nicholas, the patron saint of sailors and men at sea.

Sure enough, not long after they prayed to St. Nicholas, the wind calmed down a bit. Slowly, they were able to get the boat under control and approach an uninhabited small island named *Thea*, meaning "mother goddess."

My grandfather and the other men were so grateful for St. Nicholas's help that they promised to do all they could for him. They shouted to the sky that they would light a very big candle for him.

At last the men were able to land on Thea. They had been told there was a small church dedicated to St. Nicholas on the island, but they didn't know where it was. They spread out in different directions to look for it. After a while one of the men found the church, and then they all went there to give thanks and offer candles to St. Nicholas. In the future, they would return to keep their promise, bringing a *very* big candle, about four feet tall, as a small token of their gratitude.

Two days later, my grandfather finally arrived home. My grandmother had given up all hope of his safe return but she, too, had been praying to St. Nicholas. Soon after, when their first child was born, they named her *Nikola*. It was she who became my mother.

In keeping with her namesake, my mother has devoted her whole life to painting beautiful icons of saints. She is still doing this wonderful work of providing images that open a window to another dimension and spirit.

This true story of how St. Nicholas saved my grandfather and his friends from a terrible storm at sea is known throughout our community. Over time, it has become a living legend in Heraklion.

THE LITTLE GIRL UNDER AN OLIVE TREE

A miller, Fragiadakis Mixales, who lives outside of Zaros, Crete, told us this story about his daughter. It happened when the girl was about four years old and suffering from epilepsy:

After my daughter had had several seizures, my wife took her to our nearby St. Nicholas monastery. She laid her down to sleep just at the entrance of the monastery under an olive tree and then went into the church to pray for her healing.

When my wife returned to our daughter, the little one awoke and said, "An old man with a white beard came and touched my hand and told me, 'You are well now.'"

My daughter never had another seizure. She is married now, with two children, and lives in Athens. This true story is well known in my community.

THE BOY AT THE ST. NICHOLAS MONASTERY

The St. Nicholas monastery in Zoras, Crete, is in a remote location at the opening of a beautiful natural gorge. When we visited the priest there, he gave us coffee and tea and then invited us into his reception room. The chapel was built in the tenth century and still has some of the old frescoes of St. Nicholas. Years ago, this priest had gone there to rebuild the monastery and preserve these treasures. Here is the story he told us about another healing:

About twenty years ago, a five-year-old boy suffering from a strange incurable blood disease and edema was brought to this monastery seeking help. "The case is hopeless!" declared the best doctors in Athens. "We cannot help him."

The priest showed us a photograph of this very sick child. In it, the boy looked puffed up and very heavy, almost unable to move. He was so bloated that he could not walk in a normal manner. Then the priest went on:

The parents asked Father Chariton, whose name means "Man of Joy," for help. At his suggestion, they lay the boy on a blanket on the floor of the chapel under the fresco of St. Nicholas. Then everyone began to pray and continued to do so throughout the entire night. The next morning, the priest felt guided to instruct the family, "Don't give your son any more modern medicine."[9]

Six days later, the boy began to slim down, and his condition began to improve. The family wrote a letter to the doctors in Athens who had given up on him, saying, "Our son is getting better!" The doctors asked to examine the boy. Afterward, they reported that they had never seen such a case before. "Some nonordinary experience must have healed the boy," they said.

Now, many years later, the man who was that boy is still well and is working successfully in a neighboring town. This healing experience is quite well known to the people here. We give thanks to St. Nicholas!

Exploring Historical Sites

Other than the places just described in Greece, many more opportunities exist for exploring sites dedicated to St. Nicholas, in both the Old World and the New:

ASIA MINOR (MODERN TURKEY)

In southeastern Turkey, you can visit the ancient town of Myra—now called Demre—where St. Nicholas was Bishop and where the original church he was buried in still stands. For those unfamiliar with travel in Turkey, here are directions: Book a seat on one of the many flights that leave daily from Istanbul's Ataturk Airport to nearby Antalya, located on the southern Turkish coast. Rent a car at the airport in Antalya, for which your travel agent (who can also book a hotel in this city) can arrange in advance. Buy a road map (*karayollari haritasi*) of Turkey, and drive southwest, out of the city, on the spectacular road that follows the seacoast. After passing the city of Finike, look for a road sign on the right, indicating the road north to the farming town of Demre. As you get closer, you may see signs pointing the way to *Noel Babba*, or "Father Christmas" to the Turks. Once in Demre, you will easily locate the Church of St. Nicholas behind a shaded courtyard featuring a statue of St. Nicholas surrounded by the children of the world (as the photograph shows in our introduction). This church is

one of the most ancient in the world and has been better preserved than many ruins by the earlier restoration work of the Czar of Russia, who wanted to honor Nicholas as the patron of his country. The sanctuary still holds the small altar used by Bishop Nicholas and the semicircular seating for the clergy, with the highest place for St. Nicholas, in front of the window. A small side chapel holds his tomb. Outside the church, beautiful souvenir books are available. Nearby are several friendly outdoor cafes where it is pleasant to sit and enjoy the sunshine. The Turkish word for "ice cream" is *dondurna*. "Bottled water" is *sise suyu*.

EUROPE

In southeastern Italy, the city of Bari is the seaport to which St. Nicholas's grave was brought on May 8, 1087 A.D. That important day is still celebrated there at the Basilica, at the seaside. Right next door to it is an active fish market where the fish, including octopus, are prepared for cooking. You can easily get to Bari by train or boat. It is a good crossroads city and offers day trips to many interesting nearby villages and bustling markets. In particular, the Castle del Monte is nearby, and the village of Tulli displays a unique style of architecture that has a beehive-like appearance. Bari is an ideal destination for the more adventurous, with convenient hotels in the small towns.

In Germany, not far from the Swiss city of Basel, there are four stained-glass windows of St. Nicholas at the cathedral in the city of Freiburg, Breisgau. These stained-glass windows date from 1320–30 A.D. One of them depicts St. Nicholas calming a storm and confronting the image of the devil on a tangled sail of a ship.

Outside Paris, France, at the cathedral of Chartres, there is also a beautiful representation of St. Nicholas from the thirteenth century (as you can see in our illustration for the story, "St. Nicholas Buys a Young Man His Freedom").

If you travel in Great Britain, you can easily find a church dedicated to St. Nicholas—there are nearly five hundred of them. The most famous is likely to be King's College Chapel, Cambridge. Its choir is globally renowned for its

annual Festival of Nine Lessons and Carols on Christmas Eve, which is broadcast around the world. Near Canterbury, England, the Barfreston parish church dates back to the sixth century. In Canterbury, the Canterbury Cathedral includes a St. Nicholas Chapel in the crypt, while the cathedral in York has stained windows in honor of the saint. Also, on the southeast coast of England in Great Yarmouth you will find a historic church dedicated to St. Nicholas that is almost a thousand years old, having been finished in 1119 A.D. It offers a beautiful statue of the saint as a young man in addition to a rich history of this fascinating ancient fishing town. To get there from London, take a train from the Liverpool Station to Norwich, and then transfer to a train to Great Yarmouth.

St. Nicholas Church in Great Yarmouth, England; built in 1119 A.D. Photograph by Mr. Edward Krolak

Because St. Nicholas was known as the patron saint of sailors, most seaports throughout northern and southern Europe have churches dedicated to him, some from the twelfth century and earlier. All are likely to be considered historically significant, so any travel guidebook should list them.

NORTH AMERICA

Nicholas traveled from the Old to the New World at its outset with Columbus, who chose the saint as his patron for his first crossing of the Atlantic. Now in the United States, Canada, and Mexico there are hundreds of churches dedicated to St. Nicholas, far too many to list here. For their locations, one can simply consult local phone books variously for Catholic, Anglican, and Eastern Orthodox churches. Most of them will have paintings of the historic saint hanging on their walls. We do want to draw your attention to one site in particular:

In Beaver, Pennsylvania—thirty-five miles northwest of Pittsburgh—you will find a chapel and museum dedicated to St. Nicholas. Located at 5400 Tuscarawas Road, the chapel was built in 1992 and is a replica of several churches found in the eastern Carpathian Mountains of Slovakia. It is constructed of various hardwoods and features ten scenes from the life of St. Nicholas, each with a teaching message. The museum has many one-of-a-kind artifacts.

Finally, let us not forget that St. Nicholas is the patron saint of Manhattan! As this book's introduction mentions, the St. Nicholas Greek Orthodox Church that stood next to the World Trade Center was destroyed by falling debris on September 11, 2001. We are hoping it will soon be rebuilt for the enjoyment and inspiration of people everywhere.

Detail from Saint Nicholas with Scenes from His Life, *Russian, 16th century*

Notes

INTRODUCTION

1. See *The Oxford Dictionary of Byzantium*, ed. Alexander P. Kazhdan (Oxford: Oxford University Press, 1991).
2. See Charles Jones, *St. Nicholas of Myra, Bari, and Manhattan* (Chicago: University of Chicago Press, 1978).
3. Interview of Gian Carlo Menotti by Robert Siegel, National Public Radio's *All Things Considered*, December 24, 2001.

THE LEGEND OF THE SEAFARING PILGRIMS

4. See Jones, 17–24.
5. See Jones, 23.

THE NINE QUESTIONS

6. See Annemarie Schimmel, *The Mystery of Numbers* (Oxford: Oxford University Press, 1994).

THE LEGEND OF THE HEALING MYRRH

7. See Jones, 47, 66–73, 148 ff.
8. See Jones, 67.

AFTERWORD

9. For more information on this subject, see Ed Tick, *The Practice of Dream Healing* (Wheaton, Ill: Quest Books, 2001).

Sources

EDITOR'S NOTE: *Every effort has been made to contact all publishers and authors listed below. In the cases where we have not been able to locate them, if we are notified, we will be glad to seek permission at that time. Also, while we have made every effort to be faithful to the meaning of the original text, we have retold all translated stories with stylistic changes to enhance the narrative. For the reader's convenience, stories are listed in alphabetical order. In a few cases, where the names of the German publishers were not available, we have listed only the city and year of publication.*

"Anticipation: A Memory of St. Nicholas Day," by Anton Schnack. Translated from *Das Buch Vom Sankt Nikolaus*, ed. Nikolaus Hein (Zürich: Arche Verlag, 1962). In the original German text, the story is called "St. Nicholas Day."

"The Baker's Dozen." Dramatized by Aaron Shepard, *The Baker's Dozen: A Saint Nicholas Tale*, Reader's Theater Edition, no. 9 (New York: Simon and Schuster/ Atheneum, 1995), by kind permission of the author.

"The Beautiful Crop of Rye." Translated from Felix Karlinger and Bohdan Mykytiuk, *Legendenmärchen aus Europa* (Düsseldorf, 1967), by kind permission of Prof. Karlinger. In the original German text, the story is called "Ely and Nicholas."

"The Devil's Wager." Translated from Felix Karlinger, *Geschichten vom Nikolaus* (Frankfurt am Main und Leipzig: Insel Verlag, 1995), by kind permission of the author. In the original German text, the story is called "Nicholas and the Devil."

"The Healing Oil." Translated from Felix Karlinger, *Geschichten vom Nikolaus* (Frankfurt am Main und Leipzig: Insel Verlag, 1995), by kind permission of the author. In the original German text, this story is called "Nicholas, the Young Man, and the Healing Oil."

"The Hermit and the Mouse Maiden." Translated from Felix Karlinger, *Geschichten vom Nikolaus* (Frankfurt am Main und Leipzig: Insel Verlag, 1995), by kind permission of the author. In the original German text, this story is called "Nicholas and the Mouse."

"Holy Night." Translated from Felix Karlinger, *Heilige Zeiten: Weihnachtserzählungen aus der mündlichen Uberlieferung* (Vienna: Austrian Museum for Folklore, 1988), by kind permission of the author.

"The Icon's Warm Bread." Translated from Felix Karlinger, *Geschichten vom Nikolaus* (Frankfurt am Main und Leipzig: Insel Verlag, 1995), by kind permission of the author. In the original German text, this story is called "Nicholas and the Wonderful Bread."

"The Legend of the Healing Myrrh." Retold from Charles W. Jones, *St. Nicholas of Myra, Bari and Manhattan: Biography of a Legend* (Chicago: University of Chicago Press, 1978).

"The Legend of the Seafaring Pilgrims." Translated from Werner Mezger, *Sankt Nikolaus, Zwischen Kult und Klamauk, Zur Entstehung, Entwicklung und Veranderung der Brauchformen um einen popularen Heiligen* (Ostfildern: Schwaben Verlag, 1993).

"The Legend of Stilling the Tempest." Translated from Werner Mezger, *Sankt Nikolaus, Zwischen Kult und Klamauk, Zur Entstehung, Entwicklung und Veranderung der Brauchformen um einen popularen Heiligen* (Ostfildern: Schwaben Verlag, 1993).

"The Legend of the Three Daughters." Retold from Charles W. Jones, *St. Nicholas of Myra, Bari and Manhattan: Biography of a Legend* (Chicago: University of Chicago Press, 1978).

"The Legend of the Three Grain Ships." Retold from Charles W. Jones, *St. Nicholas of Myra, Bari and Manhattan: Biography of a Legend* (Chicago: University of Chicago Press, 1978).

"The Legend of the Three Stratilates." Retold from Charles W. Jones, *St. Nicholas of Myra, Bari and Manhattan: Biography of a Legend* (Chicago: University of Chicago Press, 1978).

"The Little Nicholas," by Winfried Wolf. Translated from *Hat der Fuchs auch eine Grossmutter?* (Ravensburg: Otto Maier Verlag, 1983), by kind permission of the author.

"Marko, the Rich Man." Translated from August von Löwis, *Russische Volksmärchen* (Jena, 1914).

"The Miller's Tail." Translated from Felix Karlinger, *Geschichten vom Nikolaus* (Frankfurt am Main und Leipzig: Insel Verlag, 1995), by kind permission of the author. In the original German text, this story is called "Nicholas and the Miller."

"The Moneybag of Molsch Talpasch." Translated from Felix Karlinger, *Geschichten vom Nikolaus* (Frankfurt am Main und Leipzig: Insel Verlag, 1995), by kind permission of the author. In the original German text, this story is called "St. Nicholas as Samaritan."

"The Nicholas Ship," by Paul Keller. Translated from *Das Buch Vom Sankt Nikolaus*, ed. Nikolaus Hein (Zürich: Arche Verlag, 1962).

"The Nine Questions." Translated from Felix Karlinger, *Geschichten vom Nikolaus* (Frankfurt am Main und Leipzig: Insel Verlag, 1995), by kind permission of the author. In the original German text, the story is called "Nicholas and the Nine Questions."

"The Pfeffernüsse." Translated from Felix Karlinger, *Geschichten vom Nikolaus* (Frankfurt am Main und Leipzig: Insel Verlag, 1995), by kind permission of the author.

"The Russian Icon: A Story from World War II," by Adolf Leopold. Translated from *Das Buch Vom Sankt Nikolaus*, ed. Nikolaus Hein (Zürich: Arche Verlag, 1962).

"The Sick King and the Simpleton." Translated from Felix Karlinger, *Geschichten vom Nikolaus* (Frankfurt am Main und Leipzig: Insel Verlag, 1995), by kind permission of the author. In the original German text, this story is called "Nicholas Heals a Sick King."

"A Small Fish Story." Translated from Felix Karlinger, *Geschichten vom Nikolaus* (Frankfurt am Main und Leipzig: Insel Verlag, 1995), by kind permission of the author. In the original German text, this story is called "Nicholas and the Fish."

"St. Nicholas and the Ant." Translated from Felix Karlinger, *Geschichten vom Nikolaus* (Frankfurt am Main und Leipzig: Insel Verlag, 1995), by kind permission of the author.

"St. Nicholas and the Monster." Translated from Felix Karlinger, *Geschichten vom Nikolaus* (Frankfurt am Main und Leipzig: Insel Verlag, 1995), by kind permission of the author.

"St. Nicholas Brings It to Light," by Ludwig Schuster. Translated from *Das Buch Vom Sankt Nikolaus*, ed. Nikolaus Hein (Zürich: Arche Verlag, 1962).

"St. Nicholas Buys a Young Man His Freedom." Translated from Felix Karlinger, *Geschichten vom Nikolaus* (Frankfurt am Main und Leipzig: Insel Verlag, 1995), by kind permission of the author.

"St. Nicholas Finds the Path." Translated from Felix Karlinger, *Rumanische Legenden aus der mundlichen Tradition* (Salzburg, 1990), by kind permission of the author.

"St. Nicholas Retrieves the Ball," narrated by H. van Noenen. Translated from Felix Karlinger, *Geschichten vom Nikolaus* (Frankfurt am Main und Leipzig: Insel

Verlag, 1995), by kind permission of the author. In the original German text, this story is called "Nicholas Helps Young Ball Players."

"St. Nicholas's Donkey," by Lisa Wenger. Translated from *Das Buch vom Sankt Nikolaus*, ed. Nikolaus Hein (Zürich: Arche Verlag, 1962).

Further Reading

Bogan, Samuel D. "The Christmas Scout." In *Chicken Soup for the Soul at Christmas*, Jack Canfield and Mark Victor Hansen, eds. London: Random House, 1999.

This is a story about a teenager named Frank Wilson, who is grieving because it is his first Christmas after his brother had been killed by a reckless driver. The story moves away from Frank's family to another part of town, where Frank becomes Santa Claus himself in an unexpected way. He had doubted that he would ever be happy again. But by following his heart, Frank finds true joy.

Dodge, Mary Mapes. *Hans Brinker or The Silver Skates*. New York: Harper and Brothers, first published in 1865.

Chapter 9 of this book tells of the coming of St. Nicholas in a nineteenth-century Dutch-American home. St. Nicholas seems to know a lot about the Brinker children and recounts in detail some of the bad things each has done in the past year. Even so, each child receives a wonderful gift. After the Reformation in the sixteenth century, when other Protestant countries were following Martin Luther's call to abandon the saints, the Dutch kept St. Nicholas very much alive. As I've already mentioned, they called St. Nicholas *Sinterklaas*, from which *Santa Claus* is said to have come.

Sidney, Margaret. *Five Little Peppers and How They Grew*. New York: Grosset and Dunlap, first published in 1881.

See chapters 16 and 17 for fun and good times. There is a wealth of warmth, love, and happiness in this home, poor only in terms of money. The older children take responsibility for making a magnificent Christmas for their

younger siblings and bringing the spirit of Santa Claus to their entire family. "Happiness like this is a blessed thing."

Wilder, Laura Ingalls. *Little House on the Prairie*. New York: HarperCollins, first published in 1935.

The chapter "Mr. Edwards Meets Santa Claus" is a heartwarming story with great suspense and feeling for frontier life at Christmas time. Laura and Mary's wonderful surprises can provide a useful outlook on the true meaning of abundance and gift giving, even today.

Selected Bibliography

Ebon, Martin. *Saint Nicholas: Life and Legend.* New York: Harper and Row, 1975.

Euw, Aloys von. *Sankt Nikolaus Begegnen.* Luzern, Stuttgart: Rex Verlag, 1994.

Hein, Nikolaus, ed. *Das Buch vom Sankt Nikolaus.* Zurich: Verlag Der Arche, 1962.

Gockerell, Nina, ed. *Weihnachtszeit Feste zwischen Advent und Neujahr in Süddeutschland und Osterreich* 1840–1940. Bäyerisches Nationalmuseum, Munich. Munich, London, New York: Prestel Verlag, 2000.

Jones, Charles W. St. *Nicholas of Myra, Bari and Manhattan: Biography of a Legend.* Chicago: University of Chicago Press, 1978.

Karlinger, Felix. *Geschichten vom Nikolaus.* Frankfurt am Main, Leipzig: Insel Verlag, 1995.

________. *Rumänische Legenden aus der mündlichen Tradition.* Salzburg, 1990.

________. *Heilige Zeiten: Weihnachtserzählungen aus der mündlichen Uberlieferung.* Vienna: Austrian Museum for Folklore, 1988.

Karlinger, Felix, and Bohdan Mykytiuk. "Legendenmärchen aus Europa." *Köln* 75: 1967.

Kazhdan, Alexander P., ed. *The Oxford Dictionary of Byzantium.* Oxford: Oxford University Press, 1991.

Löwis, August von. "Russische Volksmärchen." *Jena* 48: 1914.

Meisen, Karl. *Nikolauskult und Nikolausbrauch im Abendlande. Eline kultgeographisch-volkskundliche Untersuchung*. Düsseldorf, 1931. Reprinted with an introduction by Matthias Zender and an expanded bibliography. Düsseldorf, 1981.

Mezger, Werner. *Sankt Nikolaus, Zwischen Kult und Klamauk, Zur Entstehung, Entwicklung und Veränderung der Brauchformen um einen populären Heiligen*. Ostifildern: Schwabenverlag AG, 1993.

Nelson, Gertrud Mueller. *To Dance with God: Family Ritual and Community Celebration*. New York: Paulist Press, 1986.

Paulding, James Kirke. *Stories of* St. *Nicholas*. Syracuse, New York: Syracuse University Press, 1995.

Shepard, Aaron. *The Baker's Dozen: A Saint Nicholas Tale*. Reader's Theater Edition, no. 9. New York: Atheneum, 1995.

Wenger, Lisa. *Weihnachts Geschichten*. Aarau, Switzerland: Verlag H.R. Sauerland Co., 1952.

Wolf, Winfried. *Nur Noch 24 Tage bis Weihnachten*. Zurich: Sanssouci Verlag AG, 1984.

List of Illustrations and Credits

The editor and publisher wish to thank those who have kindly given permission to reproduce the illustrations found in this book.

Page 14: Detail from Frontispiece: *St. Nicholas with Scenes from His Life*, Russian (Tver), 16th century (tempera on panel). Richardson and Kailas Icons, London, UK/ Bridgeman Art Library, NY

Page 16: *Charity of Saint Nicholas (to the Poor Nobleman and His Three Daughters)* by Fra Angelico, 15th century (right panel of Perugia triptych, detail of the predella). Vatican Museums, Vatican State. Scala/Art Resource, NY

Page 20: *The Young Shipwright* by Robert Bruce Wallace. Mallet & Son Antiques Ltd., London, UK/Bridgeman Art Library, NY

Page 30: *Saint Nicolas*, detail of stained glass, 13th century, Chartres Cathedral, France. La Crypte, Editions Houvet, Chartres, France

Page 40: *Saint Nicholas with Scenes from His Life*, Russian icon, 16th century. Reprinted from Roderick Grierson, ed., *Gates of Mystery: The Art of Holy Russia*. Fort Worth, TX: 1992, 214

Page 56: Detail from Frontispiece: *St. Nicholas with Scenes from His Life*, Russian (Tver), 16th century (tempera on panel). Richardson and Kailas Icons, London, UK/ Bridgeman Art Library, NY

Page 58: *Saint Nicholas of Bari Liberating Three Innocent Prisoners* by Fra Angelico, 15th century. Scala/Art Resource, NY

Page 72: Saint Nicholas from the St. Reparata Polyptych (far right panel reverse) by Giotto di Bondone, 14th century. Duomo, Florence, Italy/Bridgeman Art Library, NY

Page 82: *Children on Donkey*, German card c. 1900

Page 88: Detail from Frontispiece: *St. Nicholas with Scenes from His Life*, Russian (Tver), 16th century (tempera on panel). Richardson and Kailas Icons, London, UK/ Bridgeman Art Library, NY

Page 90: Detail from *Meeting of St. Nicholas with the Imperial Messenger* and the *Salvage of the Ship with Grain* by Fra Angelico, 15th century (Perugia triptych, detail of the predella). Scala/Art Resource, NY

Page 94: St. Nicholas cookie mold, late 16th century, reprinted from Werner Mezger, *Sankt Nickolaus* (Ostfilden, Germany, 1993), 152

Page 98: *Norwegian Winterman* (color litho) by English School, 19th century. Private Collection/Bridgeman Art Library, NY

Nicholas's Church), Art Museum of Estonia, Tallinn, Estonia/Bridgeman Art Library, NY

Page 180: Detail of the Christ Child (1430 fresco) from the *Madonna delle Ombre* (Madonna of the Shadows), by Fra Angelico, 15th century. Museo di San Marco dell'Angelico, Florence, Italy/Bridgeman Art Library, NY

Page 188: *Saint Nicholas Rescuing Sailors*, contemporary icon handpainted by Christos N. Liondas. Marg. Apergi & Sons Ltd., Athens, Greece

Page 195: St. Nicholas Church, Great Yarmouth, England; built in 1119 A.D. Photograph by Mr. Edward Krolak

Page 198: Detail from Frontispiece: *St. Nicholas with Scenes from His Life*, Russian (Tver), 16th century (tempera on panel). Richardson and Kailas Icons, London, UK/Bridgeman Art Library, NY

QUEST BOOKS
are published by
The Theosophical Society in America,
Wheaton, Illinois 60189-0270,
a branch of a world fellowship,
a membership organization
dedicated to the promotion of the unity of
humanity and the encouragement of the study of
religion, philosophy, and science, to the end that
we may better understand ourselves and our place in
the universe. The Society stands for complete
freedom of individual search and belief.
For further information about its activities,
write, call 1-800-669-1571, e-mail olcott@theosmail.net,
or consult its Web page: http://www.theosophical.org

The Theosophical Publishing House
is aided by the generous support of
THE KERN FOUNDATION,
a trust established by Herbert A. Kern
and dedicated to Theosophical education.